Planet Earth
EDGE OF THE SEA

This volume is one of a series that examines the
workings of the planet earth, from the geological
wonders of its continents to the marvels of its
atmosphere and its ocean depths.

Cover
An aerial view of Captiva Island, off the Gulf
coast of Florida, evidences the ceaseless interplay
of sea and shore. The daily ebb and flow
of the tide through a hurricane-cut inlet has
deposited spreading, fan-shaped shoals of sand
that may one day form new land.

Planet Earth

EDGE OF THE SEA

By Russell Sackett
and The Editors of Time-Life Books

Time-Life Books, Alexandria, Virginia

PLANET EARTH

EDITOR: Thomas A. Lewis
Deputy Editor: Russell B. Adams Jr.
Designer: Albert Sherman
Chief Researcher: Pat S. Good

Editorial Staff for *Edge of the Sea*
Associate Editor: John Conrad Weiser (pictures)
Text Editor: Jan Leslie Cook
Staff Writers: Tim Appenzeller, Sarah Brash,
Paul N. Mathless
Researchers: Judith W. Shanks (principal),
Feroline Burrage, Ann Dusel Corson,
Sheila M. Green, Sara Mark, Reiko Uyeshima
Assistant Designer: Susan K. White
Copy Coordinators: Elizabeth Graham, Marge du Mond,
Bobbie C. Paradise
Picture Coordinator: Donna Quaresima
Editorial Assistant: Caroline A. Boubin

Special Contributor: Lynne Bair (text)

Editorial Operations
Design: Ellen Robling (assistant director)
Copy Room: Diane Ullius
Production: Anne B. Landry (director), Celia Beattie
Quality Control: James J. Cox (director), Sally Collins
Library: Louise D. Forstall

Correspondents: Elisabeth Kraemer-Singh (Bonn);
Margot Hapgood, Dorothy Bacon (London); Miriam
Hsia, Lucy T. Voulgaris (New York); Maria Vincenza
Aloisi, Josephine du Brusle (Paris); Ann Natanson
(Rome). Valuable assistance was also provided by:
Wibo van de Linde (Amsterdam); Helga Kohl
(Bonn); Lesley Coleman, Millicent Trowbridge (London); Trini Bandrés (Madrid); John Dunn (Melbourne); Christina Lieberman, Cornelis Verwaal
(New York); Mimi Murphy, Ann Wise (Rome).

THE AUTHOR

Russell Sackett is a former Senior Editor and
Chief of the Investigative Unit of *Life,* and
Washington Bureau Chief and National Correspondent for *Newsday.* He is now a freelance
writer and editor living in Seattle, Washington.

THE CONSULTANT

In 1969, Robert Dolan helped establish the Department of Environmental Sciences at the University of Virginia, where he is now a professor.
A consultant to the National Park Service and
the State of Virginia on the management and
utilization of coastal areas, Professor Dolan also
works with the U.S. Geological Survey and is
the author of more than a hundred professional
papers and books.

CONTENTS

A CONTINENT'S VARIEGATED COASTLINE

The coastlines of the world mark what naturalist Rachel Carson called "the primeval meeting place of the elements of earth and water." And, as seen here and on the following pages, the 20,000 miles of shoreline that form the boundary of the smallest continent—Australia—represent this meeting of land and sea in all its modes, from the gentle interchanges of tides and salt marshes to the brutal confrontation of waves and rocky sea cliffs.

Any shore is a place of ceaseless transformation. On sandy beaches, it may occur almost imperceptibly, as each wave sweeps a few grains of sand along the shore or out to sea. On precipitous coasts, the battle lines may shift abruptly when pounding waves chisel huge slabs from a cliff face.

The land is not always the loser. The waves that erode beaches can also extend them with sediment that is dumped into the sea by rivers, then swept along the shore by currents and deposited by the surf. And in the fecund wetlands of sheltered coasts, hardy vegetative pioneers such as the tropical mangrove build new land by stabilizing the surface and trapping sediment among their roots.

In Australia, as elsewhere, a human factor has recently entered the coastal equation. Drawn to the shore but vexed by its changeable nature, which threatens harbors and shore-front property, people constantly attempt to stabilize the shifting sands and eroding cliffs. But "the long rhythms of earth and sea" that Carson described rarely prove easy to still. Despite breakwaters and sea walls, the shore remains "a place of compromise and conflict and eternal change."

Indian Ocean swell rolls ashore at Point D'Entrecasteaux, at the southwest corner of Australia, where centuries of storm-driven seas have heaped up an expanse of sand in a broad beach backed by a field of dunes.

Cliffs up to 800 feet high front the coast of Western Australia. Exploiting lines of weakness in the limestone, the sea has hollowed and undermined the cliff face, leaving the base of the ramparts littered with rubble that will eventually be ground into sand.

The ragged contours of sandstone cliffs at Port Campbell National Park, situated on the south coast of Australia, bespeak their rapid retreat before the waves. Formed from sediment deposited on the floor of an ancient sea, the rock is being reduced to sand once again by the power of the ocean's pounding surf.

In Australia's tropical north, a river bordered by mangrove trees snakes across tidal mud flats veined with outflow channels. Like the marsh grasses of temperate wetlands, salt-tolerant mangroves of the mud flats provide a haven for a rich and varied animal life.

A pair of jetties guards the mouth of Wagonga Inlet, an estuary on Australia's populous southeast coast. Jetties and other shore-front bulwarks often interfere with nearshore patterns of water circulation, leaving nearby beaches vulnerable to erosion.

Chapter 1

FRAGILE FRONT LINES OF DEFENSE

An aerial tour of the world's coastlines would offer the observer a series of visual feasts—among them, the plunging sea cliffs of the Pacific coast of North America, the rocky, mist-shrouded headlands of New England, the steep fjords of Norway and the crescent-shaped bays of the Mediterranean. All are scenes of breathtaking beauty, and all invite meditation on the timeless workings of the sea.

Basically, these coastal landscapes owe their varying character to continual changes in sea level. No matter how the changes are accomplished—by slow fluctuations in the quantity of ocean water, by the languid drifting of the earth's tectonic plates or by sudden shifts of massive slabs of crustal material—they have a marked impact on the shoreline, which generally advances or retreats as they occur. Where not much time, geologically speaking, has passed since the most recent major change in the location of the shoreline, the land usually rises precipitously from the water's edge, and any beaches present are narrow, short, and rocky, with a scant veneer of sand. Along the Northwest coast of the United States, for instance, beaches are pocketed between rocky headlands and backed by sheer cliffs. But where the shore's location has been stable for an extended period, its rock has been ground into sand by the waves and tides, and its rugged contours have been smoothed with sand swept along the coast by longshore currents.

Where there is some protection from the wind and waves, other kinds of coastal terrain arise. Gentle tides in the sheltered waters of estuaries, which typically are river valleys drowned by a slowly rising sea, may wash mud and silt onto intertidal flats. Marine and salt-marsh plants begin to grow in the mud, and they trap more sediment until the flats, no longer vulnerable to tidal destruction, have become stable wetlands. These coastal wetlands are among the most fecund of earth's habitats, as fertile as the best farmlands; but at the same time their fragile and unusual ecology is highly sensitive to the effects of human activity.

During an airborne survey of the world's coastlines, one would often notice series of elongated islands running parallel to the shore for hundreds of miles at a stretch, like some geological basting stitch with which the ocean has been sutured to the land. These are barrier islands, appropriately named because they are the land's frontline defense against the punishment of the sea. The islands range in width from a few hundred feet to a mile, but they are invariably much longer than they are wide, and with their low profiles they appear as smooth and fragile as the bones of a bird's wing. They are found off many gently sloping coasts—along much of east-

The gentle curve of an 18-mile-long barrier beach contrasts with the indented Dorset coast of England. Though technically not an island (it is joined to the mainland at one end), Chesil beach has the low profile and the marshy shoreward lagoon typical of barrier islands.

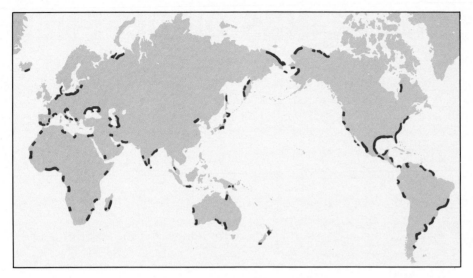

Barrier islands, shown in red on the map at left, guard some 13 per cent of the earth's coastlines. The longest stretches, totaling 2,800 miles, occur along the Eastern seaboard and Gulf coast of North America.

ern North and South America and parts of West Africa, along the coasts of India and southern and western Australia, and along most of the North Sea coast of Europe, particularly that of the Netherlands, Denmark, Germany and Poland.

In its natural state, a barrier island is a miracle of serene loveliness. The smooth, straight ocean edge is characterized by wide, sandy beaches sloping gently upward to wind-blown dunes bedecked with high grasses. Behind the dunes, in the island's interior, may be found shrubs, woods, perhaps even a maritime forest, which may abound in deer, snakes, raccoons and other wildlife. (Among America's barrier islands, Assateague Island, which lies off Virginia and Maryland, is particularly treasured because it is the home of a herd of rare wild ponies.) The shoreward side of such an island is punctuated by bays, quiet tidal lagoons, salt marshes, and—in the tropics—mangrove swamps. These wetlands provide a natural habitat for oysters and other estuarine species, and for a splendid array of marsh birds.

For many reasons, barrier islands are the most fascinating of the interfaces between the landforms and the oceans of the world. Not the least of the reasons is the seeming inequality between their frail structure and the power that the sea brings to bear against them. Nowhere is this drama played out more vividly, or on a grander scale, than on North America's East coast.

It is virtually impossible for a tropical storm or a hurricane to move ashore there without first crossing the longest stretch of barrier islands in the world, sprawling for 1,500 miles from Long Island southward to the tip of Florida. (The string of islands then resumes for another 1,300 miles along the Gulf Coast states to Mexico.) Other, more frequent assaults are made by the winter storms known as northeasters. About 30 to 40 times a year, these storms occur with enough force to scour beaches or chew into frontal dunes; of this total, perhaps three storms will be strong enough to do serious environmental damage. "And every few years," as one scientist put it, "one will come along that's a real granddaddy."

On the evening of March 6, 1962—the day before Ash Wednesday— Robert Dolan, a young graduate student from Louisiana State university, was hoping that he was about to witness such a storm. After almost three weeks of work in and around the community of Nags Head, located on the North Carolinian stretch of barrier islands known as the Outer Banks, he was on the verge of completing a research project in preparation for his doctoral dissertation on coastal processes. The aim of the research was to correlate statistics on beach changes with measurements of wave heights, currents and tides. Dolan had fastened electrically powered wave and tide gauges to a piling at the end of a fishing pier, had set bench marks at more than a dozen points along the beach and dunes, and had anchored a 25-foot aluminum camera tower on the beach near the pier for the purpose of making time-lapse photographs during daylight hours.

At day's end, Dolan left his equipment and walked up the beach to join his wife and young daughter in their rented cottage. "There was a northeaster coming up," Dolan recalled, "and I was feeling good about it. I wanted big waves and strong currents to show up in the research, and I wanted to record the build-back of the beach after a storm."

The Dolans' cottage was set back about 200 feet from the beach; a neighboring cottage, vacant this early in the season, was snugged up closer to the beach dunes. Dolan retired at about 10:30 p.m. Later, he would remember being aware of strong winds vibrating the cottage during the night. Clearly the storm he wanted was under way. He arose at 6:30 a.m., and as he prepared to shave he peered casually through the bathroom window to check the weather conditions. He promptly forgot about shaving: The foundation of their cottage was awash in about two feet of churning water, and the neighboring cottage was afloat, "moving right toward us."

Five anxious minutes later, the Dolans had packed personal belongings and research gear into their four-wheel-drive vehicle and had fled the imperiled cabin. They had a very limited choice of directions in which to go: The beach drive was flooded and virtually impassable, as was the road to the causeway that spanned Albemarle Sound and linked the island with the mainland. Most Nags Head motels were still boarded up for the winter, and in any event they were too near the water to be safe. Luckily, after driving a short distance to the south on the water-covered beach drive, the Dolans found a two-story motel displaying a vacancy sign and began banging on the doors to arouse the few off-season tenants. Water was already over the first-floor thresholds by the time the proprietor came to the door.

The Dolans and the motel occupants watched from the structure's second story as the first of the Ash Wednesday storm's incredibly high tides peaked about an hour later. The onslaught of the storm had coincided with the year's first perigean spring tide, one of the highest of the year. (The gravitational forces that cause the tides are at their maximum twice each year, when the moon, earth and sun are aligned and the moon is at perigee, its closest approach to earth.) "You could see cottages being destroyed by the waves coming over the dunes," recalled Dolan, "some of them just literally beaten to pieces by debris that was caught and swept along by the waves, hitting buildings like battering rams. There were winds of 75 miles per hour, hurricane force, and they were ripping roofs off—shingles and sheets of plywood flying everywhere."

By 9 a.m., the tide had receded enough to permit Dolan to descend for a damage check. What he saw offered little hope concerning the fate of his research site and instruments. "I couldn't see our pier, where our instruments were," Dolan later recalled, "but I had a good view of Jennette's fishing pier up the beach in Nags Head, and as I stood there watching, it just crumpled into the surf." A rescue helicopter came over to take some of

Seen from an Apollo spacecraft above the North
Carolina coast, a 200-mile stretch of the Outer
Banks barrier islands traces a fragile border
between sedimented sounds and the open ocean.

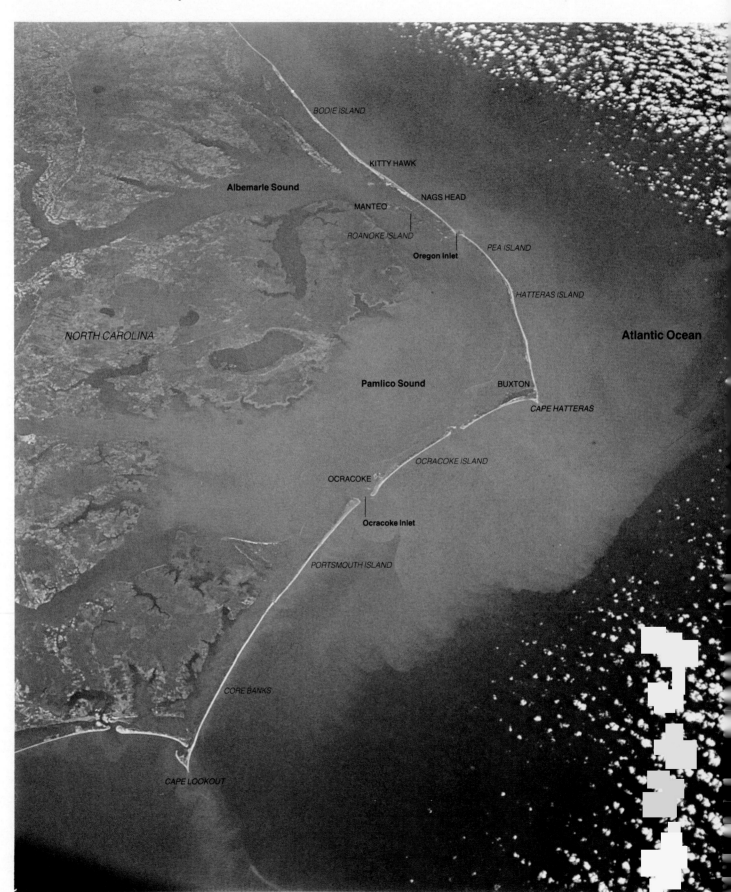

BODIE ISLAND

KITTY HAWK

Albemarle Sound

NAGS HEAD

MANTEO

ROANOKE ISLAND

PEA ISLAND

Oregon Inlet

HATTERAS ISLAND

NORTH CAROLINA

Atlantic Ocean

Pamlico Sound

BUXTON

CAPE HATTERAS

OCRACOKE ISLAND

OCRACOKE

Ocracoke Inlet

PORTSMOUTH ISLAND

CORE BANKS

CAPE LOOKOUT

the badly frightened motel guests off the island, but the Dolans stayed on. Even the low tide in the early afternoon was ominous; the waves were still running up well past normal high-tide levels. The storm was by no means over, but the low tide enabled the Dolans and others who had remained in Nags Head to get across the causeway to refuge on sheltered Roanoke Island, where efforts were being made to establish contact with islands to the north and south.

No one yet had any inkling of the storm's tremendous reach. For several days, the nation's weather forecasters had been tracking the approach of a storm—but a different one, a blizzard heading toward the coast after dumping record snowfalls on the Eastern mountain region. The prospect of a northeaster lashing the desolate winter beaches of the Atlantic seemed, by comparison, a minor matter.

Later, when they knew better, the meteorologists reconstructed the origins of the Ash Wednesday storm. It had begun in the waning days of February, after an intense high-pressure system moving southeastward from the archipelago of western Canada had brought Arctic air across Texas to the Gulf of Mexico. There, between the cold, dry Canadian system and a warm, moist maritime air mass, the cyclonic storm system had spun into existence. First noticed about 300 miles south of New Orleans, the storm moved east across the Florida peninsula on March 3, and thence slowly north and east over the waters of the Gulf Stream. By March 8, the cyclone, fueled by the warmth and moisture of the open sea, had become the largest Atlantic storm of the century.

On the mainland, the storm had remarkably little effect: It had progressed only a few miles inland when it merged with the eastbound snowstorm, contributing to the blizzard's heavy snowfalls. But on the coast, its cruel blows were felt everywhere. In Atlantic City, New Jersey, huge waves ripped up the famous Steel Pier, scene of many a Miss America pageant, and tore chunks out of the boardwalk. On Fire Island—a part of the barrier beach running along the south shore of Long Island—a front rank of beach cottages collapsed into the surf as though struck down by a huge scythe. On New Jersey's Long Beach island, an offshore barrier extending 19 miles south from Barnegat Light, the entire community of Harvey Cedars was destroyed, some of its houses sluiced by the surf clear across the narrow island and into Barnegat Bay. A mothballed Navy destroyer broke its moorings and ran aground at Beach Haven, on the south end of the barrier.

At the southern tip of Fenwick island, off the Maryland shore, the mayor of Ocean City stepped outside to assess the damage done by the storm's first high tide and discovered that the city's entire three-mile-long boardwalk had vanished. For the next two days, much of this burgeoning resort community was awash in water up to eight feet deep; more than 50 homes and apartments and 150 business establishments were damaged or destroyed. South of Fenwick island, surf raging across the barrier island of Assateague drowned scores of wild ponies as they tried to reach high ground.

On the Outer Banks of North Carolina, the storm cut a new inlet through Hatteras Island and a section of State Highway 12. In all, it obliterated more than 10 miles of Outer Banks barrier dunes that had been painstakingly stabilized during the preceding 25 years. Below Cape Hatteras, where the barrier chain bends westward, the impact of the storm waves was more oblique and somewhat less catastrophic; nevertheless, high

Aerial views of a section of Long Beach island, New Jersey, taken before *(top)* and after *(bottom)* the Ash Wednesday storm of 1962, document the erosion of the island's beaches, the obliteration of its main highway and the choking of its marshy sound with plumes of sand.

water inundated much of the island of Ocracoke. As viewed from the helicopters flying up and down the chain looking for people and wildlife in need of help, the Atlantic barrier islands were a sorry sight indeed.

Amid the horror of the storm, Robert Dolan's scientific curiosity remained undiminished. As soon as he was allowed through the National Guard roadblock on the causeway, he returned to Nags Head to see if anything remained of his research project. The 25-foot aluminum camera tower had disappeared; not so much as a single shiny fragment was ever found. Bench marks made of one-inch steel pipe that had been embedded deep in the beach now stuck up like sentinels, the sand around them having been borne off by the retreating surf. Dolan was able to locate the pier piling where he had mounted his wave gauge and, remarkably, found the gauge and its scroll graph still there and the graph still legible; it showed that electric power to the pier had failed just after the gauge had registered a wave measuring 18 feet in height.

As relief and rescue workers, engineers, National Park Service rangers, resort developers and homeowners slogged glumly through the devastation of the Ash Wednesday storm, the scope of the damage that had been done to the Atlantic barrier islands gradually became apparent. Beaches were gouged back to the dune line, which in many instances had itself disappeared. On narrow islands such as Assateague, the green vegetation behind the dune line had been smothered in overwash fans of sand, the imprints of the huge waves that had broken over the dunes. Along sections of the Outer Banks, the dunes had been stripped back to expose the spines of sand fence that had been installed 30 years before, during the Depression, as part of a dune-enhancement program. Sound-side docks were obliterated by overwash sediment, and lagoon channels were choked with sand and debris. Whole islands appeared to have been warped and buckled beyond recognition; the National Ocean Survey hurriedly set about revising coastal navigation maps. Sickened by the destruction, many beach-property owners and developers prepared to liquidate what remained of their holdings.

But sand retains few scars to remind people of its instability, and building soon resumed on the Atlantic barriers. Wherever the owner of a damaged or destroyed home decided a location was too risky, someone else was more than eager to take over the spot. The splintered cottages of the Fire Island beach front were replaced with expensive contemporary structures suitable for the covers of architectural publications. Atlantic City, on its way to becoming the gambling capital of the East, rebuilt its boardwalk and piers, and within a few years gained new hotels, restaurants, and highrise apartment buildings. In Ocean City, Maryland, the frame structures that had been smashed off the beach front by the storm were replaced with a row of towering condominium apartment buildings arrayed along the beach in the very area the storm surge had covered to a depth of several feet.

The desire for an ocean view—a desire so powerful as to sweep aside much cautionary evidence of the sea's destructive ways—is an old story in America. Not long after the end of the Revolutionary War, Philadelphians who were wealthy enough to own private yachts adopted the custom of sailing down Delaware Bay to an anchorage at the southern end of New Jersey—off a barrier island called Cape May. By 1801, an enterprising postmaster had opened the nation's first resort hotel there; the modest, one-room structure

During the Ash Wednesday storm of 1962, waist-deep waters shear houses from their foundations in the barrier-island community of Harvey Cedars, New Jersey. A photograph taken several days later *(inset)* shows the extent of the storm's destruction.

The Losing Battle for the Beaches

The efforts made by civil engineers to save eroding beaches with multimillion-dollar projects are, at best, temporary solutions that often hasten the destruction of the shoreline.

Many developed beaches bristle with groins and breakwaters, bulwarks meant to revitalize an eroding strand by trapping the sand that is carried along the shore by longshore currents. But for every beach thus broadened, another farther down the coast shrivels, its sand supply cut off.

Sea walls are constructed just behind the shoreline to check the retreat of the beach and to protect waterfront structures from storm waves. However, sea walls are among the most destructive works of shoreline engineering. At Atlantic coast resorts such as Cape May, New Jersey, and Miami Beach, Florida, waves rebounding from sea walls have chewed away at prized beaches far more quickly than natural erosion ever did.

A SEA WALL
A broad expanse of beach (*top*) becomes narrower and steeper (*center*) after a sea wall installed at the base of the dune line prevents the waves from replenishing the beach with sand that would otherwise be washed down from the dunes. In the meantime, waves breaking with full force against the artificial barrier scour away more and more sand until the sea wall itself becomes undermined (*bottom*).

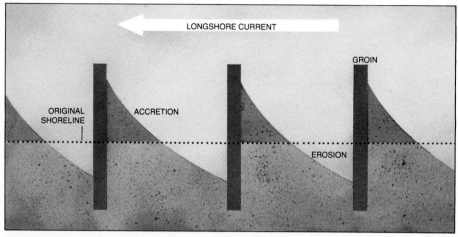

GROINS
A series of groins juts out from a beach, catching sand swept along the coast by longshore currents. A broad crescent of beach accumulates upcurrent of each one of the groins, but behind the groins the shoreline is starved of sediment and recedes.

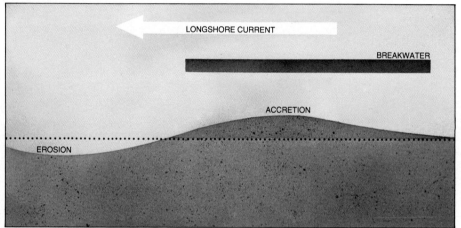

A BREAKWATER
Built hundreds of yards offshore, a breakwater creates a wave shadow, a region of calm where the sand that is carried along the shore settles, adding to the adjacent beach. But the downcurrent beach, now deprived of its sediment supply, quickly erodes.

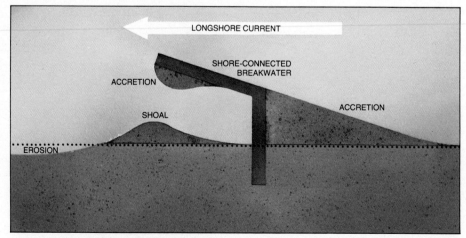

A SHORE-CONNECTED BREAKWATER
Sediment collects along the upcurrent face of the breakwater and forms a shoal in the pocket behind it, which is protected from the action of the waves. No longer nourished by sand deposited by the longshore current, beaches farther along the shore erode apace.

was soon followed by boardinghouses and private homes occupied by business owners, socialites and legislators until, by the middle of the century, Cape May was a thriving resort town.

The resort towns that began to appear in the United States and elsewhere during the 19th Century were creatures of the Industrial Revolution. The mechanization of work left people with leisure time; increased productivity boosted their incomes; and the rise of the railroads provided the means of traveling previously unthinkable distances to spend time relaxing at the shore. An additional impetus was the widespread belief that the shore was a healthy place (the curative powers of salt water and sea air had been touted by European doctors long before America came into existence).

All along the Eastern Seaboard of the United States, buildings appeared closer and closer to the waves. In 1920 the permanent residents of Miami Beach, Florida, numbered 644; a decade later there were ten times as many. Meanwhile, Atlantic City had entered its golden age as the East Coast haunt of café society; in 1930 its population reached an all-time high of 66,000. Inevitably, property damage done by storms became more frequent and more expensive, fostering the very impulse that the legendary King Canute had shown to be futile—to do something to hold the sea in check.

The engineers who were enlisted in this task proposed measures already in use on mainland beaches: protective walls of concrete or rock built out into the surf. These projects included jetties to keep sand from accumulating in channels and inlets, and groins to slow the wave-driven currents that run along the shore. The idea of the groins was to encourage the sand carried by these longshore currents to settle and remain on the beaches, and the structures did in fact cause sand to accumulate on their upcurrent sides. But a drawback soon became apparent: With the sandy cargo of the longshore current artificially depleted, the beaches on the downcurrent side of the structures were deprived of replenishment and began to erode at an even faster pace than before.

A typically frustrating effort was made after a 1933 hurricane opened an inlet just south of Ocean City, Maryland, dividing one long barrier island into two—Fenwick island and Ocean City to the north, and Assateague Island to the south. The U.S. Army Corps of Engineers constructed jetties on both sides of the new channel to maintain it for boat traffic, and in so doing ensured the ruin of Assateague Island's northern end. The beach south of the inlet, deprived of sand, shriveled until it was no longer even connected to the jetty.

With beaches still disappearing, engineers often turned to sea walls to absorb the impact of storm waves before they could overwash the dunes and further cut back the beach. Much later, it was noticed that their effect was invariably to steepen and diminish, rather than protect, the sandy shore.

A last-resort technique for stabilizing barrier beaches is replenishment: A shoreface is rebuilt by pumping dredged sand onto it. This method is not intended to be permanent; the relocated sand enters the shore-current system and eventually, like the sand it replaced, disappears from the beach. Replenishment is generally less costly than the construction of barricades; but maintaining a beach this way requires frequent reapplication of sand, and lasting success is expensive. In the late 1970s, Miami Beach, whose once-famous strand had vanished from in front of its sea walls, allocated $64 million to a 10-year beach-replenishment program.

Finding the sand for repeated replenishment of a barrier beach can be a serious problem. Sand from bays and lagoons behind the islands is finer than beach sand and often disappears rapidly in the surf. Dredgers in search of coarser ocean sand have had to venture as far as two miles offshore. When the sand has been located, transferring it from the offshore portion of the beach system to its upper face raises a new problem, because the operation unnaturally steepens the profile of the beach. Wind and waves promptly set to work to return the beach to its natural shape, so the erosion of the beach face is accelerated and replenishment is soon required again.

For many years, the barrier-island stabilization program that seemed most promising was the restructuring of the frontal dunes along North Carolina's Outer Banks. One of the early concerns was the protection of State Highway 12, planned to run from the causeway at Kitty Hawk all the way south to the town of Ocracoke, a distance of approximately 90 miles. Beginning in 1933, two Depression-born federal agencies—the Civilian Conservation Corps (CCC) and later the Works Progress Administration (WPA)—combined forces with the National Park Service to anchor some 600 miles of sand fence along the beach-front dunes of Bodie, Pea and Hatteras Islands. The aim was to trap sand in a high barrier dune running along the face of the Outer Banks. These superdunes were further stabilized with the planting on their rear slopes of beach grasses and some 2.5 million trees and shrubs.

The results were striking: The augmented dunes soon loomed above the

The broad swath of beach, low dunes, and sparse vegetation of Core Banks, one of the Outer Banks of North Carolina, typify a barrier island in its natural state. Most storm waves spend their force harmlessly on the long, low beach, reshaping the shoreline but renewing the island's interior with sediment.

A bulwark of artificial dunes rises behind the beach at Ocracoke Island, north of Core Banks, where a program was implemented in the 1930s to stabilize the sand with fences and a carpet of fertilized grass. Since then, stormy seas breaking with full force on the dune line have steadily eroded the beach sand.

beaches, their comforting bulk encouraging vacationers and motel owners to build just behind them. What no one yet understood was that the buttressing of the beach dunes would eventually bring on more trouble than it would prevent.

At the time that its dune-enhancement program was begun, Hatteras Island closely resembled Core Banks, an undeveloped barrier island that lies south of Ocracoke. Fifty years later, Core Banks, accessible only by boat, was virtually unchanged, its beach a broad expanse of sand varying in width from 325 to more than 600 feet, its foredunes low, its vegetation relatively sparse, and the salt marshes on the sound side of the barrier lush and extensive. It was the archetypical barrier island. But in the same period of time, Hatteras became much narrower and higher, with foredunes reaching an elevation of 30 feet in some stretches. It also became far greener than Core Banks, because the higher dunes protected the dune grasses and shrubs from the adverse effects of salt spray and overwash. The Hatteras beaches, once as much as 650 feet wide, had receded to a width of 100 feet or less and had steepened appreciably, while the sound-side marshes, deprived of replenishment from overwash, had also narrowed.

When first formulated in the 1930s, the dune-stabilization policy had been greeted with widespread enthusiasm; a typically laudatory article appearing in *Science News Letter* in 1937 was headed: "Man-Made Sand Dunes Saving Carolina Seashore." But in 1963, after the Ash Wednesday storm, attitudes toward the program began to change, and the advocates of dune building began to hedge. Park Service Director Conrad Wirth told a Congressional hearing that dune stabilization would not be completed "for at least another 10 or 12 years." He added, however, that when the dunes were finally restored, "the shore will start building out again." But the beach continued to retreat, and by 1966 the Park Service tacitly admitted that stabilization was not working; it resorted to a replenishment program and began pumping new sand onto the Outer Banks beaches. In 1968, a new Park Service Director, George B. Hartzog, warned Congress that it was "saddled forever with the cost of beach nourishment."

Earth scientists had come to understand by that time that there was in fact no way to change the natural forces at work on the barrier islands, no matter how much engineering was put into place. But until the Ash Wednesday storm had so dramatically demonstrated the vulnerability of these coastal landforms, few people in either government or the private sector were interested in what the scientists had to say. After the storm, the dawning realization that there were not enough dollars in the entire national budget to stabilize the barrier islands prompted a renewed search for sensible answers.

Robert Dolan helped lead the search. His firsthand experiences in the storm transformed him from an occasional critic of established policy into a hard-driving advocate of a new attitude toward the eternally shifting coastline. Partly because of the heightened interest of the time in all ecological

Birth of a Barrier Island

The barrier islands that rim the world's coastlines are moving monuments to the last ice age. Scientists disagree on what sequence of events gave birth to these changeable ribbons of sand, but they know the process started with the melting of the great ice sheets and the consequent global rise in sea level that began some 15,000 years ago.

Three scenarios of how the barrier islands were assembled are illustrated at right. The most widely held theory is that dune lines on the mainland were slowly surrounded by the advancing sea. In another view, the islands began as large sandbars and were moved slowly up the continental shelves by sand-laden waves breaking in shallow water. A third possibility is that most barrier islands are relics of sandspits built out from the mainland by longshore currents, then severed by storm-cut inlets.

Whatever their origin, the barrier islands share a remarkable characteristic: They are by nature mobile, and by constantly trundling shoreward keep just ahead of the relentlessly rising sea.

ORIGINAL
SEA LEVEL

A FLOODED BEACH
A line of dunes fronting the coast during the Ice Age *(top)* is marooned, forming a barrier island, when the sea begins to rise as the ice sheets melt *(center)*. As the ocean continues to advance, the island migrates up the continental shelf *(bottom)*.

issues, his message of respect for natural processes began to gain wider acceptance; as Dolan later said, it was a case of "the right storm at the right time in the right place."

Most geologists believe that the barrier islands owe their existence to the ice ages. Time and again during the long history of the earth, mile-thick sheets of ice have spread outward from the polar regions, eventually to recede again. Each advance has corresponded to a marked cooling of the earth's climate, and each withdrawal has been accompanied by a warming trend. During the ice ages, so much water was trapped in the massive glaciers that sea levels dropped by hundreds of feet and the continental shorelines were extended seaward. During warmer periods the glaciers melted, the seas were replenished and the coastlines retreated inland. The process is a lengthy one; the rise of the world's oceans that began at the end of the last ice age, between 12,000 and 15,000 years ago, continues to this day.

The most widely accepted explanation of the genesis of the barrier islands takes the conclusion of the last ice age as its starting point. Swelled by meltwater from glaciers, the rising seas slowly began to inundate the coastal plains of the world, pushing ahead of them masses of debris, mud and sand. The wind winnowed out the sand and began to pile it up in dune ridges parallel to the shoreline. During storms, the long sand ridges were breached by pounding waves, and sea water pouring through the inlets flooded the

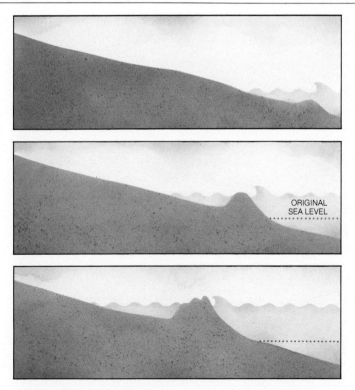

AN EMERGENT SANDBAR
A submerged sandbar develops (*top*) as waves approaching the shore stir up and deposit sediment from the bottom of the ocean. Eventually, the bar crests the waves (*center*) and begins to migrate toward the shore as a full-fledged barrier island (*bottom*).

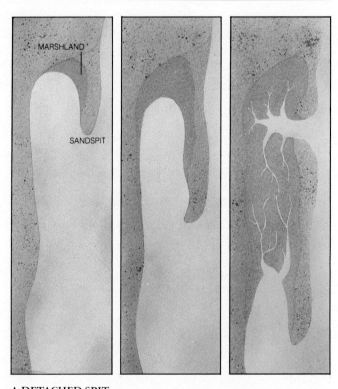

A DETACHED SPIT
A current coursing along the shore piles sediment in the lee of a promontory, building a sandspit and a tract of marshland (*above, left and center*). A storm eventually opens an inlet through the spit, leaving a barrier island backed by a marshy lagoon (*right*).

nearly flat land behind the ridges. The former dune ridges thus became a series of isolated segments completely surrounded by water—the first barrier islands.

For many years, scientists assumed that the islands formed more or less where they are today. But most now think that the barrier islands originated at the edge of the continental shelf, and that as the sea rose and the shoreline retreated inland, the barriers migrated to their present positions. The barrier islands off the Carolinas may have migrated 40 or 50 miles, those off the coast of Georgia nearly 80 miles, and some of the islands in the Gulf of Mexico as much as 100 miles. Moreover, since the sea level continues to rise at a rate of about a foot a century, the barrier islands are still migrating, a recently recognized phenomenon that has profound implications for the islands' inhabitants. Migration is, in fact, essential to the continued existence of the islands, since it is only by moving inland, up the gentle slope of the coastal plain, that they remain above the rising sea level. Geologists now realize that a variety of natural forces, ranging from delicate breezes to awesome storm surges, conspire to accomplish this remarkable, ponderous movement.

Sea breezes continually waft sand from the beach across the dunes to the rear of the island, gradually shifting the entire dune chain. As the dunes retreat, their former bases become the beach. During severe storms, the process is accelerated; waves breaking over the tops of the dunes wash huge fans of sediment inland, and from this sediment the wind creates new dunes. Sand that is washed still farther back, into the marshes at the rear of the island, builds the marshes into solid land. Pushed even farther back into the bays and lagoons behind the marshes, the overwashed sand becomes new marshland. Sometimes, storm waves break completely through a low spot on a barrier island, depositing great quantities of sand in fan-shaped shoals or shallow deltas in the lagoons and bays. Eventually the inlets close again, and the deltas are joined to the main body of the island. Sand is also moved through an inlet out into the open ocean from the bay, but this sand tends to be dispersed along the front beach by longshore currents; the net build-up near an inlet is invariably on the back side of a barrier island.

The transport of sand from the beach and foredune to the back of the island changes the island's contour and position, but not its total sediment mass. The island in effect rolls over itself, in a movement that has been compared to that of the treads of a military tank. This explains the mysterious presence of peat deposits and stumps of ancient trees on the front beaches of some islands; they are remnants of marsh and maritime forests that once flourished on what used to be the other side of the island. While its features are dissolved and re-formed, the island's identity remains unchanged, a sandy proof of the maxim of the Greek philosopher Heraclitus: There is nothing permanent except change.

In the late 1960s, scientists began to campaign for a reconsideration of government policy on the barrier islands. Robert Dolan, then at the University of Virginia, and Dr. Paul J. Godfrey, a biology professor from the University of Massachusetts, began urging Park Service officials to stop pumping money into dune stabilization. As Godfrey put it, enhanced barrier dunes do not protect a beach but "can be thought of as agents for enhanced beach erosion."

The Shifting Sands of Grand Gosier

Nowhere is the protean nature of barrier islands more apparent than along the Gulf coast of the United States, where frequent hurricanes—an average of one each year—can reshape the sandy shore in a matter of hours. One extremely fragile barrier found there is Louisiana's Grand Gosier island, a five-mile-long ribbon of sand that rises little more than four feet above sea level and is only a few hundred feet wide.

More substantial barrier islands often weather storms with little sediment loss; the waves that carry sand away from the beaches strew it across the interior of the island. On Grand Gosier, though, heavy seas and storm surges often roll uninterrupted across the island, carrying much of the beach irretrievably into the sound.

Three times in the past 20 years, large portions of the island have been reduced to shoals, marked only by breaking waves. In 1965, Hurricane Betsy scoured a broad inlet through the northern part of the island. Four years later, the eye of Hurricane Camille brought a storm surge that submerged Grand Gosier under some 15 feet of water and left just five tiny islets showing above water level. In 1979, the onslaught of Hurricane Frederic obliterated the southern portion of the island.

But immediately after each episode of destruction, slow shoreline processes begin to rebuild the ravaged island with waveborne sediment. Just two years after Frederic, the southern extreme of the tenacious Grand Gosier had reemerged as a pair of beaches.

Aerial photographs of Grand Gosier island, in chronological order left to right, trace 16 years of storm-wrought transformations. The first was taken in October 1965, just after Hurricane Betsy; the second in April 1969, before Hurricane Camille; the third in June 1980, after Hurricane Frederic, with shoals marking the site of the southern island; and the fourth in September 1981, after two years of rebuilding.

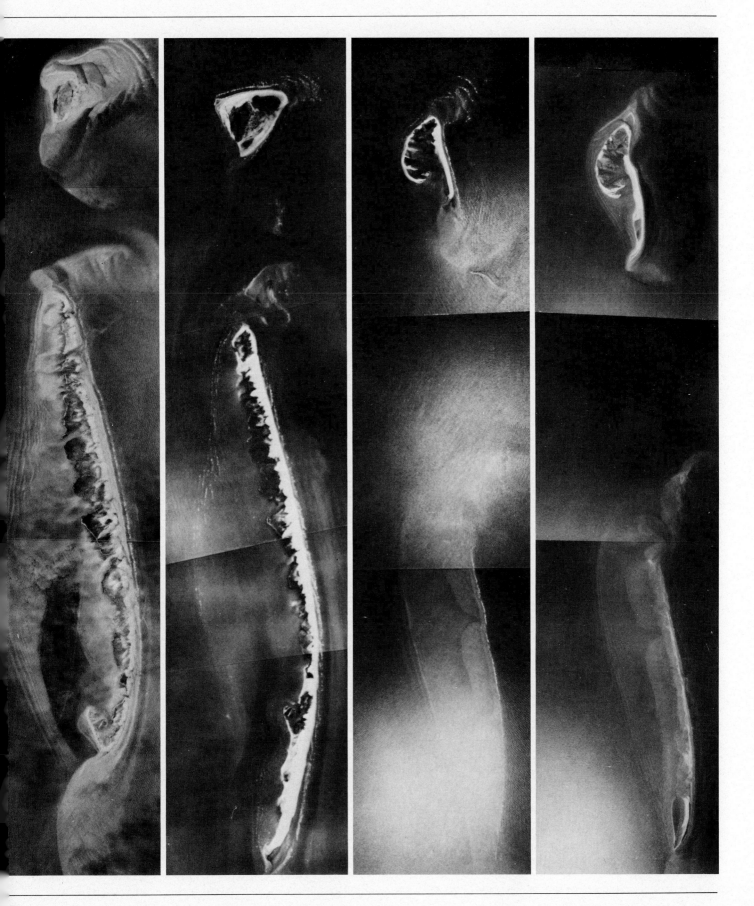

The remains of a forest that once grew on the landward side of Capers Island, South Carolina, are battered by the surf; centuries ago, the forest was

covered with sand by the island's ceaseless rolling migration toward the mainland, then emerged on the ocean side for this final phase of destruction.

Vacation homes on Kiawah Island, South
Carolina, clustered a prudent distance away
from the changeable shoreline, epitomize
a sensible approach to beach-front development.

Where the frontal dunes of an island are built up enough to prevent inlet
formation and overwash, they interfere with the equilibrium of the island
environment. Beach erosion increases because the unnaturally high dunes
reflect wave energy and prevent sand deposition on the beach by the waves.
Erosion accelerates on the back side of the island because the dunes block
the storm-wave overwash that builds new land behind the dunes. The natural roll-over of the island is interrupted, and its ability to migrate is
destroyed. Eventually, as the sea level continues to rise, the ocean will
overtake the immobilized island. In a study done for the Park Service, Dr.
Godfrey described overwash as part of the barrier island's "intrinsic mecha-
nism for surviving enormous oceanic forces."

This sort of talk was strong medicine for residents of Outer Banks communities long accustomed to equating overwash with property damage and
personal danger. The attention given the theories of Dolan and Godfrey
suggested to one county commissioner that the federal government, in its
eagerness to drop the expensive dune-stabilization program, would "let our
school buses be trapped by Godfrey's overwash."

Faced with the evidence that its massive erosion-control program was
not going to work, the Park Service began to edge cautiously toward a
new policy—letting nature take its course. Officials were extremely reluc-
tant to discuss the ramifications of such a change, and in fact the policy
switch was never actually announced; it leaked out and was quickly spread
by environment-conscious media. To the surprise of the Park Service, how-

ever, nationwide public response to the change was highly favorable.

After 1973 the Park Service did not, except in a few emergencies, stabilize another dune. And by 1978, the superintendent of the Cape Hatteras National Seashore felt comfortable enough to make an unequivocal statement of seashore-management strategy: The National Park Service, he said, "will not attempt to stabilize any part of the federally owned shoreline, will consider each inlet that opens and/or closes on a case-by-case basis, and will allow natural processes to shape and change individual dunes and dune systems."

Robert Dolan and his colleagues believe that, as a consequence of the change in Park Service policy, Cape Hatteras will return to its natural state by the year 2000, and parts of Nags Head, Kitty Hawk and other towns will be overtaken by the sea. As the artificial dune dike built during the 1930s is allowed to give way, new foredunes will form along the ocean, and secondary dunes will absorb the impact of the advancing surf. Where storm waves do wash sand across, it will start fragile new marshes and eventually build new land.

One prominent element of the Cape Hatteras landscape will be secured against the sea—the lighthouse that warns ships of shallow waters and treacherous currents. When it was built in 1870, it stood 1,500 feet from the beach; 100 years later, migration of the island had left it less than 150 feet from the surf. The Interior Department plans to keep the lighthouse from falling into the ocean by surrounding it with a revetment that will retain an island around the structure as the barrier island gradually moves on. Within about 100 years, the fortified light will be completely detached from the main island and will stand off to sea, as one authority has observed, "like a beacon to the whole lesson of migration."

Thus, there are strong indications that the government and private owners are learning to live with the restless barrier islands. Unfortunately, coping with the random catastrophe of a major storm is more of a problem. No location and no structure on a barrier beach can be considered entirely safe during a major storm, and the danger has been growing for several decades. Seaside resorts have burgeoned: By the 1980s the population of Miami Beach, for example, approached 100,000—more than triple its prewar level—while the number of winter visitors topped one million. In the same time period, the number of severe storms along the East Coast increased markedly, as did the length of the winter storm season and the duration of the average storm. Furthermore, the rise of the sea level continues; between 1920 and 1975 it amounted to one foot.

Spurred by these multiple threats, Dolan and his colleagues at the University of Virginia have developed a system for recording and analyzing physical changes in the contours of the Atlantic barrier shoreline from New Jersey to South Carolina. Every five years, various federal agencies have worked together to photograph the entire chain of islands from the air. The researchers then assemble continuous-strip photographs of the 650 miles of Atlantic coastline, divided into 90-yard sections for close study. Each section is carefully scanned for contour changes, which are recorded and analyzed by computer. Among other things, the analysis has shown that the islands that face northeast erode more quickly than those with more southerly exposures. It also strongly suggests that storm-hazard zones along the coast occur in a regular pattern, and that sections of shores that have taken serious erosion and storm damage in the past may very likely go through it again in the future.

In the opinion of most coastal authorities, another midwinter storm comparable in intensity to the Ash Wednesday storm would do many times the $500 million damage and cause many more than the 32 deaths that occurred in 1962. Noting the growth of population and commercial activity along the Atlantic and Gulf Coasts, geographer Gilbert White has called these areas the most likely sites of future catastrophic events. On the subject of hurricanes, most authorities are even more specific in their warnings: Richard A. Frank, former administrator of the National Oceanic and Atmospheric Administration, says, "a hurricane will kill hundreds, if not thousands, of Americans and cause billions of dollars of property damage sometime soon. I do not know precisely when or where, but it will happen." **Ω**

Atlantic surf breaks near the base of the 208-foot-tall Cape Hatteras lighthouse, the loftiest in North America. By 1980, the advancing sea had whittled away more than 1,400 feet of beach and dune since the construction of the lighthouse, well inland, in 1870.

RAMPARTS OF ROCK

Where there is no broad beach to buffer the assault of the sea on a coastline, waves quickly strip the land to bare rock. Unlike resilient beaches, which are gradually regenerated after being pared away by storm damage, rocky coasts have only two modes of confrontation with the sea: temporary resistance and catastrophic retreat.

The continuing worldwide rise in sea level caused by the melting of Ice Age glaciers is moving most coastlines inland. Thus, most sea cliffs are relatively recent features, and the processes that shaped them can still be seen at work.

As waves attack the slope of a rocky coast, they gradually cut a horizontal notch at the water line, leaving a submerged terrace below. When rubble accumulates on the terrace, waves batter the wall of the notch with the gravel and pebbles, speeding the destructive process. Rock that is patterned with cracks yields to a form of erosion called quarrying; wave impact rams water and air into the gaps, splitting off large slabs. Waves can attack the rock only at water level, but as rockfalls trim away overhanging sections, the nascent sea cliff moves slowly inland.

The contours of coastal cliffs depend on the kind of rock present and on variations in the ferocity of the waves. Basalt, granite and other hard rocks can form sheer cliffs rising 1,000 feet and more, while softer rock, planed by constant landslides and worn by wind and rain, may meet the water in a gentle slope. Rocks of uniform hardness sometimes yield straight, unbroken walls of sea cliffs. But most coasts are scalloped, with coves hollowed out of softer rock and headlands of more resistant rock jutting into the waves.

Ultimately, the sea can cut back the coast so far that the broad terrace left at the water line saps the energy of incoming storm waves and protects the sea cliffs from further erosion.

Basalt columns guard the coast of Sudero, in the Faeroe Islands of the North Atlantic. The ancient upwelling of magma that formed the rock fractured as it cooled, creating a rock structure that is readily quarried by waves.

The weathered grain of ancient granite is
exposed at Land's End, England. Wave action
and rockfalls have gradually worn away
the cliffs along the fracture planes of the rock,
leaving craggy turrets and battlements.

Layers of tuff—compacted volcanic ash—
slope gently to the water's edge on the island of
Oahu. Wind and rain planed the tuff above
high-tide level while the waves eroded it below.

Sedimentary Cliffs under Siege

The erosion of a coast of soft sedimentary rock such as chalk or conglomerate can be dramatically swift. The retreating sea cliff can truncate the coastal landscape, cutting deep into forests and fields while leaving outcroppings of more resistant rock far behind on the wave-cut terrace. In 1810, storm waves undermined sections of the chalk cliffs of Dover (*right*) so quickly that the resulting landslide shook houses several miles away.

Vulnerable to wave attack, cliffs of soft rock also succumb to other forms of marine erosion. Limestone and chalk actually dissolve in sea water, a process that can slowly riddle sea cliffs with grottoes and tiny coves. And marine organisms, such as rock-boring clams and sponges, sea urchins and certain kinds of algae, can pit and abrade the rock at the water line, stealthily undercutting a cliff even in calm weather.

Some of the most striking shore-front sculpture results from the combination of terrestrial and marine erosion. Wind, rain and seeping groundwater can carve a rocky shore from above, even as the sea chisels it from below.

Chalk cliffs slice through seaside ridges and gulleys near Dover, England. The sea quickly consumes rubble dislodged by waves and landslides, exposing the cliffs to wave attack and ensuring their continued swift retreat.

An outcrop of weathered limestone on the coast of Yasawa, in the Fiji islands, was undercut not by waves but by the solvent action of sea water and by burrowing marine organisms.

Trees perch atop a sea stack, isolated when the softer portions of the gravelly conglomerate of Hopewell Cape, New Brunswick, eroded around it. Waves have already notched the base of the stack and will eventually topple it.

Ridges of striated limestone form a seaside maze on New Zealand's South Island. Originally covered with earth, the highly soluble limestone was etched by groundwater before breakers stripped away the soil and bared the rock to erosion by waves and weather.

Chapter 2

ARMIES OF SAND ON THE MARCH

Somewhere high in the Alps, a bit of rock crumbles from the bank of an icy stream and slips into the rushing water. Thousands of miles away, in Oregon, the mighty Columbia River plunges out of the forested Cascade Mountains bearing a torrent of debris—remnants of fallen trees, chunks of rock dislodged from the mountainsides, silt from stream beds. In this fashion, pieces of the earth from every part of every continent begin a long, watery journey that will see them winnowed and ground, assembled and eternally reshaped in the shifting, almost fluid landforms that are known as beaches.

Depending on their origins, beach materials can be extravagantly colorful. Black sands derive from old lava flows, white sands from the shells and skeletons of trillions of assorted marine organisms (the legendary beaches of Tahiti are dazzling white on the leeward side of the island, black on the windward side). The dark gray-green sands of the beaches along the Oregon and Washington coasts can be traced to huge basaltic eruptions that covered the plateaus several hundred miles inland some six million years ago and were eroded and carried down to the Pacific by the Columbia River.

The size of the materials that make up beaches may vary considerably. Sand is the most familiar component, but England's Dover Beach and much of the French Riviera consist of bits of flat gravel called shingle, and larger stones—cobbles—are the chief constituent of the glacial beaches of Alaska. Many geologically young beaches exhibit a progression of textures, from a narrow strip of sand next to the surf, through zones where cobbles and boulders abound, to sheer cliffs. Such arrangements are found in some of the pocket beaches that indent the steep shorelines of Oregon and Washington.

The older the beach, the more material has been accumulated and the finer it has been ground. The stretch of broad, ancient beaches along the Atlantic coast of the United States consist of sand that began as sediment eroded from the cliffs of the Blue Ridge and Appalachian mountain ranges and washed down to the seas millions of years ago by rivers such as the Susquehanna, the Hudson and the Delaware. The rivers deposited the heaviest fragments close to shore; the finer ones were carried out to deep water and settled on the continental shelf. Some of these deposits were nudged slowly back toward the shore by wave action, eventually riding the surf onto the beach. Today the mountains have been worn down to a fraction of their former size, and the rivers move ponderously across the coastal plain, depositing their sediments in estuaries such as the Chesapeake Bay. Atlantic

Foaming surf gently caresses its handiwork, a beach at the foot of the sheer sea cliffs of northern California. Waves, the master builders of beaches, pound rocky headlands to sand and sweep in sediment from offshore to shape these ever-changing buffers.

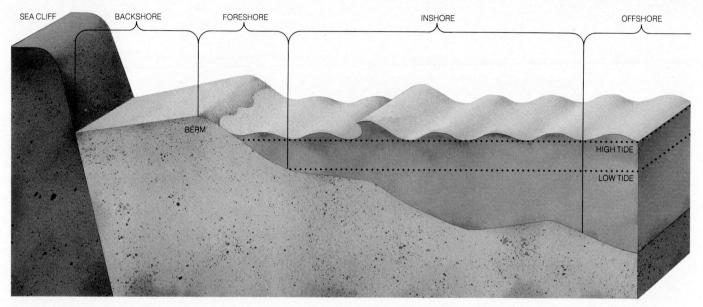

SEA CLIFF   BACKSHORE   FORESHORE   INSHORE   OFFSHORE

BERM

HIGH TIDE

LOW TIDE

beach sands are now replenished mostly from the vast reservoir of ocean-bottom sand, with some new material added by the waves that attack and slowly crumble the rocky headlands of the New England coast and the sandy coastal bluffs to the south.

In the main, these Atlantic beach sands consist of light-colored quartz and feldspar—the most weather-resistant and chemically stable of all the constituent minerals of the original rocks. After millennia of weathering and traveling, only a few dark grains remain of the unstable heavier minerals, such as hornblende, garnet or ilmenite, that demonstrate the sand's ancient origin in the inland mountains. The farther south one goes along the Atlantic coast, the greater is the proportion of sand that consists of the bleached skeletons and shells of tiny marine animals. The powdery white beach sands of southern Florida consist almost entirely of fossil shell fragments; the average age of the fragments is 13,000 years.

Along the northwestern coast of North America, large quantities of beach sand are being supplied by swift rivers falling from relatively high mountains, but a considerable amount of sand is also being manufactured by the action of the powerful Pacific waves on rocky headlands. Storm waves undercut a cliff, causing it to collapse into the surf, where the rubble is pummeled eventually into sand.

The seemingly fixed landform known as a beach is in fact a dynamic entity. In the course of a single day it narrows and widens with the advance and retreat of the tides. From week to week, other changes occur: Early in the summer the texture of the beach at a certain distance from the edge of the water may be softer and more yielding than it was a little earlier. The reason for this is that a new layer of sand has been delivered by the ceaselessly working waves, which are in the process of gradually widening the beach.

When compared from season to season, these incremental changes can add up to dramatic contrasts. In summer the beach at Carmel, California, is more than 200 feet wide; in the autumn it begins to retreat, losing as much as five or six feet a day until, by midwinter, its fine white sand has essentially vanished. Within a couple of months, however, the beach begins to rebuild, and by July it is once again as wide as it was the summer before.

When marine geologists speak of beaches, they are usually referring to much more than the narrow, shifting strip of sand above the water level.

The shifting mass of sand that constitutes a beach is shaped by wave action into four distinct areas. The backshore zone and the beach berm it encompasses are beyond the reach of most waves; the foreshore is constantly washed by the surf. The inshore zone is where the waves break, and the offshore region extends beyond the breaker zone to the depth at which the incoming waves begin to stir up sediment from the bottom.

Willard Bascom, director of the Southern California Coastal Water Research Project, defines a beach as "all sand in motion above and below water out to a depth of about thirty feet," where wave action no longer has any major effect on the bottom. Beaches, he says, can be thought of as "armies of sand particles, always on the move." In cross section a beach is a wedge of sand that tapers seaward through the intertidal zone to a point beneath the sea's surface. Under the water there are often ridges of sand, called sandbars, which are also intrinsic parts of the beach's dynamic system.

But the story of a beach extends much farther to sea than bars. Practically everything that happens to a beach is achieved through the agency of waves. They are a fascinating phenomenon in their own right.

Almost all waves owe their birth to the wind and are driven by gravity. As the wind passes over a water surface, friction and drag prevent the water from flowing along with the moving air; instead, the water piles up into crests. The wind exerts even more force against the inclined surfaces of the crests and tends to push them higher at the same time that gravity is acting to flatten them. The result of the contesting forces is an energy pattern that moves through the water, in the words of one authority, "like a shiver in the skin." Individual particles of water move upward into the crest, forward and downward as the crest passes, then backward and upward almost to their original positions as the crest is replaced by a trough.

A beach made up of weathered boulders lies exposed at low tide near Nelson, New Zealand. The rocks, some of them measuring as much as two feet across, were riven from a nearby ocean-front cliff by waves and then were nudged along the shore by currents in a slow journey that smoothed and rounded them.

The stronger the wind and the greater the expanse of open water, or fetch, that is affected by it, the higher the crests of the waves it generates. The shoreline of the Pacific Northwest is afflicted by breakers of extraordinary power and size—as documented by events at a lighthouse perched on Tillamook Rock, just offshore and a bit south of the Columbia River's mouth. The sheer walls of the compact rock island rise some 90 feet above the water, and the light itself rises nearly 50 feet higher. In one December storm, a 135-pound rock was thrown right over the top of the light; it landed on the roof of the keeper's house, demolishing the interior. In 1912, a keeper checking on a strange hoarseness in the sound of his foghorn found it choked with small rocks. The horn was 95 feet above normal sea level.

For all their drama and their sudden dislocations, storm waves are infrequent contributors to the crafting of shorelines. Most of the work is done most of the time by a remarkably regular procession of waves marching ashore far from their place of origin.

When waves move away from areas where they are born, they tend to smooth out into regular undulations called swell. Winds and waves from other storms may amplify or diminish the swell, but once generated, it husbands its energy so efficiently that it can persist across thousands of miles of open water. When the swell reaches the shoaling waters of a continental shelf, a complex series of interactions begins; their net effect is to release the waves' energy at last and turn it to the work of sculpting coastlines and beaches.

Waves begin to touch bottom while still miles from shore. This is because the rotary motion of the water particles at the surface induces similar movement in the underlying water. The diameter of the orbit described by a water particle at the surface is equal to the wave height, the distance from the top of the crest to the bottom of the trough. Similar cycles are repeated by the water underneath, but with rapidly diminishing diameters, to a maximum depth of one half the wavelength—the distance between the successive crests. Average swell along the Atlantic coast, moving shoreward at 20 to 25 miles per hour with a wavelength of 250 to 350 feet, begins to be affected by the bottom in 125 to 165 feet of water.

The results are manifold; the bottom begins to interfere with the orbital movement of the wave, with immediate consequences for both the surface swell and the bottom itself. The forward movement of the waves is slowed down; the waves bunch up and their crests become steeper. In addition, the movement into shallower water tends to align the waves; if a wave approaches the shore at an angle, its leading edge will be slowed down in the shallows while its farther reaches catch up, and the entire wave will tend to bend until it approaches the shore head on. This is one of the reasons why the long-term effect of wave action is to straighten a shoreline.

In a seeming paradox, the water particles within the wave form begin to rotate faster even as the forward movement of the wave form slows. Their orbits are squeezed into a smaller, more elliptical shape and they complete each revolution faster. As a result, the effect of the water movement on the bottom sediments is greatly increased.

As the water becomes shallower, the particles have more and more difficulty completing their circular movement. Meanwhile, gravity is acting constantly to level the wave, and soon there is not enough returning water

Foaming surf laves a beach of black sand on the island of St. Vincent in the West Indies. The sand, evidence of the island's volcanic origin, was eroded from regions of jet-black volcanic rock, then washed onto the beach by waves and offshore currents.

53

available to fill in the crest and maintain the symmetrical shape of the swell; the waves steepen and assume a peaked, rather than rounded, shape. Usually this occurs just before the water reaches a depth of about 1.3 times the wave height; then the wave becomes so unstable that it collapses, or breaks.

The unsupported top of the wave crest falls forward, entrapping air bubbles to produce the white foam that is characteristic of breakers. Now the behavior of the wave is utterly transformed, and the water itself moves along with the wave form in what is called a wave of translation. Overcome at last by gravity, the wave flattens and makes its last headlong rush up the shoreface, marking its ultimate end with a line of thin, foamy swash.

The slope of the bottom just offshore determines the nature of the breakers above it. Where the slope is gentle; the surf generally takes the form

Tilted layers of sandstone and clay, vividly colored by iron salts, pattern the cliffs of Alum Bay, on Britain's Isle of Wight *(below)*. The variously hued beach sands that have eroded from the cliffs are sold in souvenir shops *(right)*.

of spilling breakers, which peak gradually and break in a cascading line of foam that slides down the face of the wave. If the final approach to the shore is steep, plunging breakers occur; this type of breaker curls forward and topples as an intact mass of water. On a very steep slope, the breakers start to curl over as if to plunge, but then the base of the wave outruns the crest up the beach and the wave collapses into itself (*pages 58-59*).

The strength of the wind also affects the shape of waves, of course, and accounts for momentary and seasonal changes in the beach. A steep, plunging storm wave creates a sudden backwash as it breaks, and it strips a large quantity of sand from the beach as it returns to sea. The stronger winds and more frequent storms of winter produce waves that are generally higher and closer together. There is not enough time between waves for the water carried onto the beach to sink into the sand, and the berm—the familiar strip of sand that is usually dry in summer—is continually saturated. The swash frequently runs right over the top of the berm and deposits more sand at its crest before receding, thus raising the berm's height. As the water rushes back down the beach face, it skims off a layer of sand as it goes. In this way, the beach is steadily built higher at the crest and cut away along its face; it is steepened and narrowed at the same time.

Although the winter waves are stronger than those of summer, they are still not strong enough to strip away all the material of the beach. Only the finer sand grains are carried, in turbulent suspension, back into the sea; the heavier pebbles or cobbles are dropped back onto the beach. The steep, narrow winter beach is therefore also rough and cobbled. Sandy beaches usually have a slope of nine degrees or less; beaches that have a slope of between 10 and 14 degrees are customarily covered by coarse sand, and beaches with slopes exceeding 15 degrees are usually composed of gravel or shingle.

While the withdrawal of finer sands steepens the visible beach face, it has the opposite effect on the shoreface beneath the surf, which is flattened as the raked-back sand is spread across it. This longer, shallower approach then acts to protect the shore; it causes the winter waves to break sooner, dissipating their final impact against the beleaguered berm.

A winter beach blunts the assault of the waves in another important way. Frequently the backwash of the breaking waves carries sand seaward into the breaker zone, where the sediment is deposited in the form of offshore ridges, or bars. Often more than one bar is formed, and these, with their intervening troughs, act as a sort of washboard-like baffle system, slowing the rampaging advance of the waves.

As spring brings a gentling of wave action, the erosion process goes into reverse: Lower, slower waves ease the sand from the offshore bars back onto the berm; as summer progresses, the bars are moved closer to shore, diminished and sometimes completely removed, having been incorporated in the summer beach.

Thus, although every winter storm brings apparent destruction of the shoreline, the seasonal variations are natural consequences of the dynamic equilibrium between the beach and the sea. Left to their own devices, the waves and the armies of sand enact an ancient and self-perpetuating confrontation that has no winner and no loser.

The exchange of sand between the onshore and offshore zones of the beach

is straightforward for many enclosed beaches, such as the pocket beaches of Oregon and Washington and parts of the California coast, but on most coastlines it is affected by another important factor: the longshore, or littoral, current. This movement of water along the shore, generated by waves that approach at an angle, transports sand from one end of a beach to another or to a different beach farther down the coast and builds sandspits and longshore barriers.

A road in ruins testifies to the implacable power of the waves that shape the shores of Half Moon Bay in California. A breakwater built nearby in 1962 accelerated erosion; since that time, the surf has quarried away the cliff face at up to 20 feet per year.

The Danish oceanographer J. Munch-Petersen has likened the work of the waves and longshore currents to that of a combination excavating machine and conveyor belt; the waves excavate the sand and drop it onto the conveyor belt of the currents, which move it along the shore. The currents do not have to move very swiftly, and sand need not move very far with each wave, in order for a tremendous quantity of sand to be carried over a remarkable distance; on an average day, some 14,000 waves may strike the beach, each moving a few grains of sand a quarter of an inch for a total distance of perhaps 250 feet. During a storm, the grains can move more than 1,000 feet a day. Research by the U.S Army Corps of Engineers has shown that the longshore currents off Sandy Hook, New Jersey, move 436,000 cubic yards of sand per year; off Santa Monica, California, the annual volume of sand relocated by the currents is a million cubic yards.

Sand is carried until the longshore current is slowed or deflected by inlets, bars, headlands or man-made structures such as groins and jetties. Then the sand begins to settle and accumulate. Where coastlines are irregular, as they are along much of California, the waves and long-shore currents have a straightening effect, distributing the sand in the pockets between headlands and sweeping it across the mouths of bays into long spits. Eventually the headlands are cut back, the scalloped pocket beaches are filled out, or the bays become closed off as spits are extended across them.

Beaches depend on the littoral conveyor belt for replenishment. Sand that is moved from one beach will soon replenish another beach downcurrent. Nevertheless, natural changes in the shoreline often threaten human activities and property values and, as has been the case on the barrier islands, the response has often been misguided. Artificial devices engineered to mitigate the workings of the waves and currents almost always have an opposite long-range effect.

A notable demonstration of this irony was supplied by Bay Ocean, one of the most ambitious Pacific resort developments of the early 20th Century. Bay Ocean was built on a spectacular timbered spit at the mouth of Tillamook Bay on the Oregon coast. A cruise ship and special trains were to convey vacationers from Portland and other cities along the coast to enjoy the resort's paved streets, sumptuous hotel and natatorium, or swimming palace, with its heated salt-water pool.

The spit began to erode, and the idyll along with it, after a jetty was built to create a stable inlet through which ships would be able to enter Tillamook Bay. The jetty deflected the powerful longshore currents that had supplied the dunes on the spit with copious quantities of sand. The jetty was extended in 1932, and the dunes eroded even faster, at a rate of six feet per year. When the beach had disappeared entirely, the Pacific Ocean began cutting away at the peninsular cliff itself. First the hotel, then the natatorium began sliding into the sea. In the winter of 1939, a severe storm tore an inlet through the spit, leaving what remained of the resort stranded on an island; the only road leading to Bay Ocean halted suddenly at a chasm 50 feet wide.

Wind-generated waves are not the only kind that alter a beach. Every day, the beach is changed from a narrow strip to a broad expanse and back again by the grandest waves of all—the tides.

Like every other wave, a tide has a crest, a trough, a wavelength and a period, the length of time it takes a crest to travel one wavelength. But for the tides, the dimensions of two of these features are colossal: The period of a tide is 44,700 seconds, or 12 hours and 25 minutes, and its wavelength is half the circumference of the earth.

Whether the crest and trough of the tide, familiar to us as high and low tide, are noteworthy features depends upon one's frame of reference, for tidal range varies enormously around the world. Indeed, some oceanographic authorities have speculated that one of the major reasons that Western scientists did not even begin to study tides until comparatively recently is that early civilizations arose around the Mediterranean Sea, where the tidal range is so slight that it is of little interest. Willard Bascom has commented: "Not until a number of explorers had ventured beyond the Gates of Hercules into the Atlantic and observed tides in England, where the range is large, was the relationship between the phases of the moon and the height of the tide established. Then some fifteen

THE MAKING AND BREAKING OF A WAVE

Gently rounded waves of ocean swell can travel for thousands of miles across open ocean, continuing their journey with almost no change of shape or diminution of energy long after the wind that originally raised them has died away. But as they approach a shoreline, waves are transformed in distinctive ways by a complex sequence of events that begins far below the surface of the water.

The tugging of the wind that generates a wave sets water particles rotating upward into the wave crest, down again into still water and back almost to their starting places. Only the form of the wave, not the water itself, travels forward. But the orbiting particles set others below them in motion until the water is affected to considerable depths. When a wave is still far from land, its turbulence begins to graze the seabed. At first the only result is that the wave crests steepen and bunch together. But as the water grows shallower, the water particles soon can no longer complete their orbits fast enough to fill out the form of the wave as gravity draws it irresistibly onward; finally the wave is overcome, and it breaks.

Breakers, which may spill, plunge or surge, depending on the steepness of the underwater slope, release the energy hoarded during the waves' oceanic voyage. Their foamy death not only drives the pulses of swash that skate up the beach face, but also contributes to the cycling of currents within the breaker zone. These wave-driven flows often travel parallel to the beach in what are known as longshore currents; and inevitably they return seaward, sometimes in concentrated and powerful rip currents. Moving vast quantities of sand, the swash and nearshore currents continually reshape the beach as they spend the last of their waveborne energy.

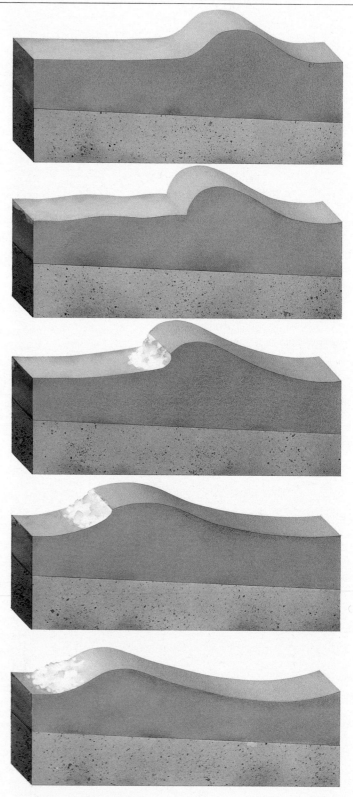

A SPILLING BREAKER
When a wave rolls across a gently sloping bottom into ever shallower water, it gradually steepens along its shoreward face until its crest begins to spill into the trough ahead of the wave in a leisurely cascade that slowly drains away the energy of the wave.

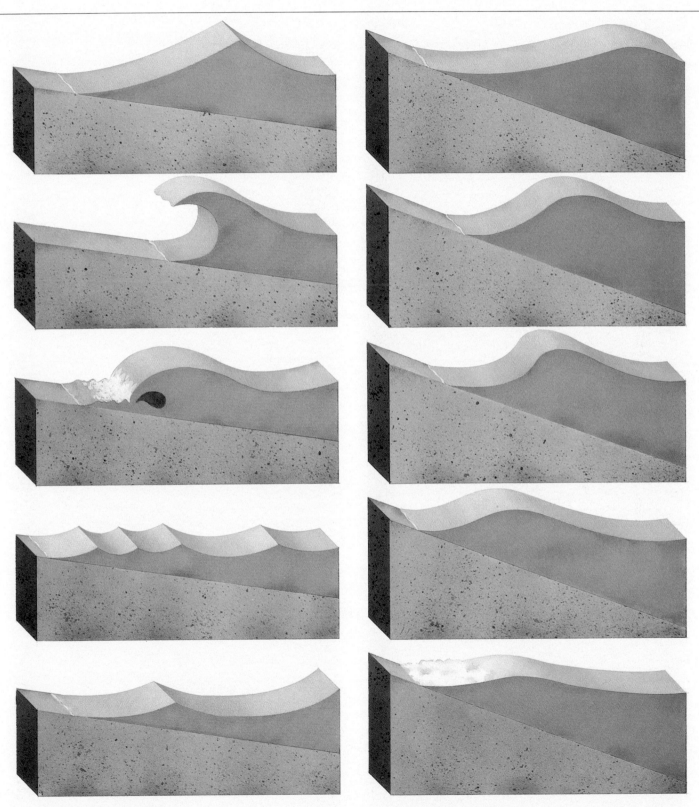

A PLUNGING BREAKER
On a steep beach, a wave quickly meets water too shallow to sustain
its advance. Its crest arches forward unsupported, collapses around
a pocket of trapped air, then rushes up the beach in what are known
as waves of translation before retreating as backwash.

A SURGING BREAKER
On a beach that is very steep, an incoming wave heaves up sharply in
the abruptly shoaling water, and then collapses into itself as the
base of the wave outruns the crest, surging up the beach in a foamy
sheet of swash that undermines the wave form.

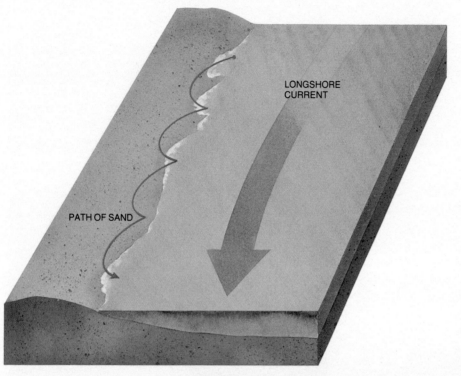

LONGSHORE FLOW

Breakers approaching the shore at an angle push the water along parallel to the beach in a longshore current that can carry large quantities of suspended sediments. Meanwhile, pulses of swash from the breaking waves move grains of sand along the beach in a series of small arcs.

A RIP CURRENT

When water swept inshore by surf is trapped behind a submerged obstacle, such as a sandbar, it may return seaward in a powerful, narrow flow known as a rip current. Fed by currents moving along the shore, a rip current may cut its own channel in a sandy bottom or follow a permanent cleft in a rocky shoreface.

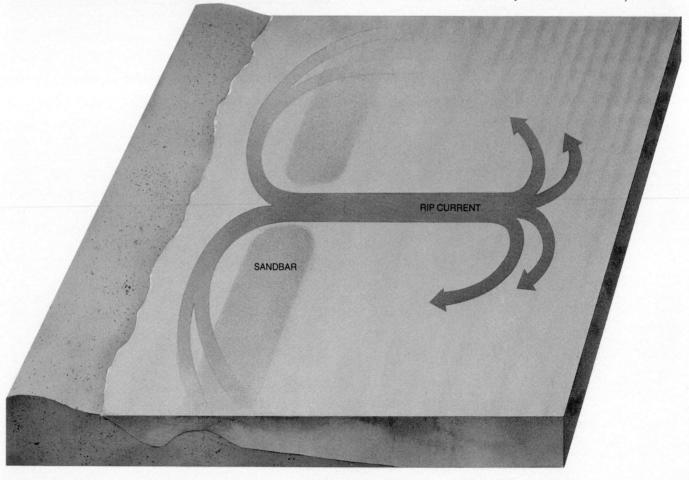

hundred years passed before Johannes Kepler wrote of 'some kind of magnetic attraction between the moon and the earth's waters'—and Galileo scoffed."

Kepler was essentially right; the gravitational pull of the moon and the sun on the oceans causes the tides. The moon, being much closer to the earth than the sun is, exerts a far greater attraction, pulling toward it the water on the nearer side of the earth. The gravitational pull on the water exceeds the centrifugal force acting on the orbiting planet and raises a tidal bulge, or wave. On the other side of the earth, because the effect of gravity drops sharply with distance, centrifugal force exceeds the pull of the moon, and the result is a tidal bulge on that side as well. These tidal bulges, or waves, maintain their positions relative to the moon as the earth rotates. Moving across the face of the sea, they wash most ocean shores with two high tides, or wave crests, and two low tides, or wave troughs, every day. Because the moon is also moving—in the same direction as the earth rotates—the actual interval between the tides is 24 hours and 50 minutes.

The sun also causes two such tidal bulges, but because it exerts much less gravitational attraction, they are very slight. However, twice a month the earth, moon and sun are aligned and the sun's gravitational pull adds to that of the moon. This arrangement, called syzygy, occurs when the moon is in its full and new phases, and it causes higher-than-usual high tides, called spring tides. At the same time, low tides are lower than normal. When the moon, earth and sun form a 90-degree angle, the gravitational bulge produced by the sun occurs in the trough of the lunar tides, diminishing both the high and low tides by about 20 per cent. These tides, which occur when the moon is in its first and last quarters, are called the neap tides.

Other permutations of this basic pattern further exaggerate the tides. Because the moon's orbit around the earth is an ellipse, approximately once a month (every 27.55 days) the moon is at its closest point to earth, or perigee, and the oceans' lunar bulges are accordingly somewhat higher than normal. Periodically, perigee occurs at the same time as syzygy, producing a still higher tide called a perigean spring tide. Occurring at least once every six months, these are normally the highest tides of the year and often coincide with the most destructive storms (the Ash Wednesday storm of 1962, for one).

Tides are barely observable until they reach the continental shelf and begin to show the influence of its basins. The usual tidal range in the open ocean is less than two feet, but the nature of the tide waves changes as they pass landward over the continental shelf, rising and slowing somewhat as they make contact with the ocean floor, as though they were headed up a ramp. The response of tidal advances to contact with the shelf varies according to the shape of the basin. The configuration of the shelf and coast may act to amplify the tide range or to diminish it; great variations in the range may be found within short distances of each other. The Panama Canal provides one example of such a tidal anomaly. On the Caribbean side, the tide range is only about one foot. Fifty miles away, on the Pacific side of the same waterway, the tide range averages 14 feet and may be as much as 21 feet at spring tide.

At the mouth of the Amazon River, the incoming tide presents a truly

A breaker that may have originated in a storm thousands of miles distant arches forward to spend its energy on a Hawaiian beach.

spectacular sight. Funneled inward by high dikes at the river's mouth, the advancing tide causes a sudden upheaval of the water into a steep, breaking front called a tidal bore. It has been described as "a several-miles-long waterfall traveling upstream at a speed of twelve knots for three hundred miles." The accompanying roar can be heard 15 miles away. Tidal bores occur wherever the tide is constricted by long, narrow estuaries or river banks. Among other famous bores are those of the Severn River in England, the Tsientang River of China, and the St. John River of New Brunswick, Canada. Although the bores are only a few feet high, they provide a mesmerizing spectacle: Nothing else in nature is like them.

Every organism that dwells within the reach of the tide must be able to survive in both water and air. A barnacle colony may be submerged in a cool tidal pool at dawn and exposed on sun-baked rocks at noon. Because the alternate exposure and drenching are not random but rhythmic, intertidal creatures have been able to adapt to their peculiar circumstances with great success. Various kinds of plants and animals, making different accommodations to the lengths of time that a particular level of the shore is covered and uncovered by the sea, have segregated themselves into zones, often providing a visible imprint on their preferred habitat.

Although these zones are established primarily by the tides, other factors are at work. Foremost among them is the character of the shore: The intertidal organisms that survive by clinging to rocks and boulders would not be able to establish a foothold on the incessantly shifting surface of a sandy beach. Exposure to the open sea, or protection from it, also determines what forms of life can survive on the shore. Some animals and plants are far more able than others to withstand the pounding of the surf. The seaweed or rockweed called wrack is a case in point. Wracks abound on rocky shores. One Atlantic species, the knotted wrack, can survive only on shores that are protected from heavy surf, and indeed the knotted wrack dominates the plant life of shores where gentle swell does not tear its elastic strands. On less sheltered parts of the North Atlantic shore, the knotted wrack is replaced by the bladder wrack, which has greater tensile strength in its strands and so can withstand the attack of heavier surf. But not even the bladder wrack can take the pounding and pulling of the waves along shores that are completely open to the ocean, and on such exposed rocky beaches there is no wrack at all.

Intertidal animals and plants are also confined to certain areas of the beach by the activities of other life forms along the shore. Barnacles, for instance, are restricted to a narrow band on a rocky shore. Above this band, the more prolonged exposures to air would kill them, and on the seaward side the barnacles are ousted by mussels and wracks that are competing for the same territory. A single frond of wrack, with its constant sweeping undulation in the waves, can prevent barnacles from taking hold in a wide area.

Some voracious animals of the lower shore restrict the range of other creatures by a more direct means: They eat the intruders that venture too close. For example, on Tatoosh Island, just off the coast of Washington, mussel beds cover the rocks in the middle of the intertidal zone. They go no higher because they could not stand the longer interval out of water, and even though partial submersion suits them, they extend no farther into the sea. The reason can be clearly seen at low tide: rows of great purple or orange sea stars—popularly known as starfish—that feed ravenously on submerged mussels, prying the delicate shells open with their rows of strong feet. The longer the mussels are underwater, the more likely they are to provide a meal for the starfish. And in fact, when the sea stars were removed from Tatoosh Island by a research scientist at the University of Washington, the mussel colonies edged a few feet lower down into the intertidal zone.

Scientists are by no means agreed on exactly what determines the zonation of many species. Nonetheless, shores all over the world share a basic pattern of life that is governed essentially by the stages of the tide, or more precisely, by the environmental conditions the tides create. To living creatures, the withdrawal of the sea brings exposure to heat or cold, desiccation, drastic swings in salinity (higher when the sun evaporates the water from a tidal pool at low tide, lower when a sudden rain dilutes a salt-water pool), and withdrawal of the food supply brought by the sea—microscopic organisms, bits of plants, animal remains and other debris. And for the animals that breathe with gills, extracting oxygen from water, ebb tide means a reduction of accessible oxygen.

With the coming of high tide, the parched life of the shore is bathed in the restorative water of the sea, cooled or warmed by its moderate temperature, revitalized with its fresh supplies of food and oxygen, and resupplied with the sea's unique gift of salt. But the arrival of the tide also means exposure to the action of the waves, whether they take the form of a

Marooned at ebb tide, boats sprawl on the harbor floor at Lynmouth, on England's Bristol Channel. The variation between low and high tides at Lynmouth can approach 30 feet, a range typical of coasts where channels or narrow bays amplify the tides.

gentle lapping or a furious pounding. These are the conditions that govern the survival and distribution of the animals and plants that live in the intertidal zone.

On a rocky shore, the first sign of the sea is what appears to be a black stain high on the rocks. It marks what is sometimes referred to as the splash zone, an area beyond the reach of the highest tide, wet only by rain and the salt spray of the waves below. The strange dark discoloration, a clear, continuous band on the rocks, consists of millions of tiny plants, most notably black marine lichens (other brightly colored lichens may provide flecks of orange or green) and blue-green algae, which are among the most primitive of all plants. The tiny algae are enclosed in slimy cases that protect them from dehydration by the sun and air, and make the surface of this threshold to the sea a slippery one when wet.

Just below the dark band but still in the zone wet only by rain, splash and spray, the cracks and crevices of the rocks hold the first creature that has unequivocal ties to the sea: the tiny littorine snail, or periwinkle. Most littorines still lay eggs in a capsule that floats in the sea; however, they have almost made the transition from sea creature to land animal, for they obtain some of their oxygen by breathing air (one European species has no gills and will drown if constantly submerged in water).

Although periwinkles will die if they dry out completely, they can stand long periods of drought; one species, the rough periwinkle, can endure up to 31 days of exposure to dry air. The periwinkle survives in such inhospitable conditions because it can close its operculum, a kind of trap door to its shell, when it senses that it is starting to lose water. Enclosed in a tiny reservoir of its own making, the creature waits until a new supply of moisture becomes available. It cannot breathe while it waits, but another of its talents is the ability to shut down its body functions until it can open its trap door again.

Not many other creatures can withstand the rigors of the splash zone for long. A few terrestrial insects that do not object to an occasional bath in salt spray crawl about among the rocks, as does the sea slater, a marine cousin of the wood louse. But for the most part, the high, rocky shore presents a rather barren face. Only after a storm does it abound with life. Then numerous land and sea animals may scurry about, scavenging among the litter of seaweeds and animal remains that are left behind by the waves.

On virtually any rocky coast, the high-tide mark is established by the presence of white acorn barnacles, one of the most ubiquitous of intertidal creatures. The white zone begins at the highest of high tides and is usually sharply defined, because barnacles never colonize above it. There is more difficulty in establishing a lower level for the barnacles, for they are found in profusion well down the shore, even in areas where they are underwater most of the time.

An array of barnacles somewhat resembles a honeycomb, or perhaps a field of miniature volcanoes. Remarkably adapted for survival on the surf-dashed rocky shores of the high intertidal zone, each small creature has an encasement that is concrete-hard and perfectly contoured to deflect the force of waves. The barnacle is cemented so tightly to the rock that it can be removed only with the aid of a strong, sharp blade.

A Shore's Stratified Society

Although just a few yards wide, the narrow seacoast strip between highest and lowest tides spans a broad range of environments, classified by scientists into four so-called life zones. These zones, distinguished by characteristic plants and animals, are present on all the tide-washed coasts of the world, from the tropics to the polar regions.

In the photograph at right, the life clustered on a rocky shore forms distinct bands of color, created by the organisms that predominate in each zone. The diagram details the creatures that typically occupy a rocky coast in a temperate climate; it also shows the stratification that tends to occur within each life zone.

The topmost zone in the sequence, the splash zone, is dampened only occasionally by spray from the highest breakers. It is the most barren of the strata, for intertidal life consists mostly of marine creatures ill suited to long exposure to the air. Lichens and blue-green algae give the band its characteristic dark color. Below the splash zone, bounded to landward by the level of the highest tides and extending down to the average high-tide mark, lies the upper intertidal zone, which is washed by tidewater only several hours a month. Barnacles, massed in a white band, are this zone's most visible tenants.

A bluish band of mussels marks the beginning of the middle intertidal zone, flooded and exposed twice daily by the tides. And at the very bottom of the intertidal region, bared only a few hours each month by exceptionally low tides, lies the low intertidal zone, lush with kelp plants and richly populated by organisms unable to weather more than a brief exposure to air.

The four intertidal life zones, with their concentrations of different organisms in bands along the shoreface, are schematically shown at right and are clearly seen in the photograph, which portrays the rocky shore of Tatoosh Island, Washington, at extreme low tide.

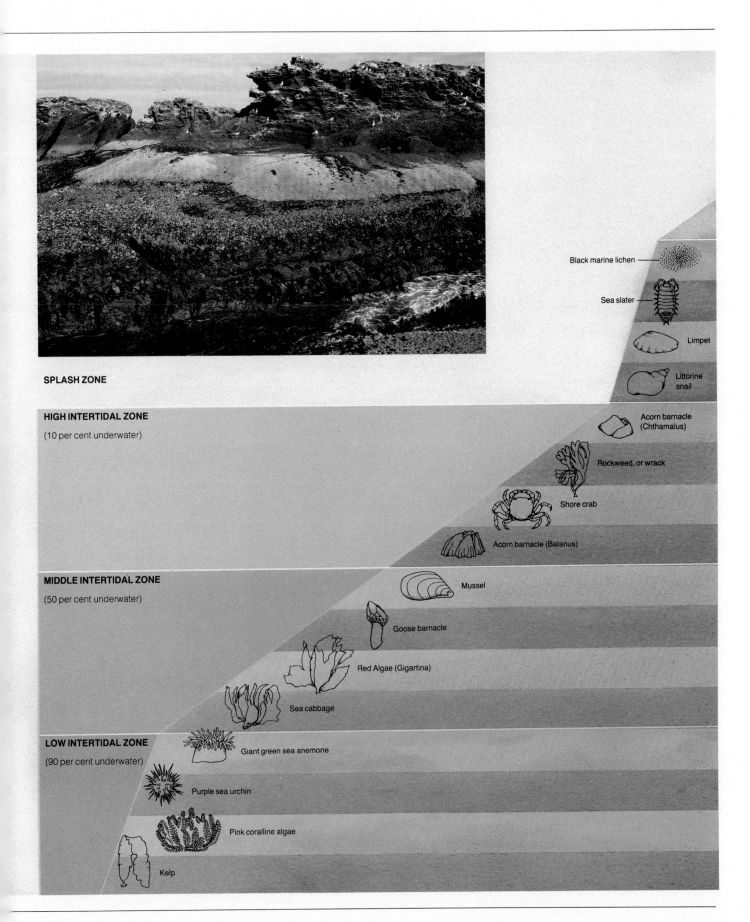

Black marine lichen

Sea slater

Limpet

Littorine snail

SPLASH ZONE

HIGH INTERTIDAL ZONE

(10 per cent underwater)

Acorn barnacle (Chthamalus)

Rockweed, or wrack

Shore crab

Acorn barnacle (Balanus)

MIDDLE INTERTIDAL ZONE

(50 per cent underwater)

Mussel

Goose barnacle

Red Algae (Gigartina)

Sea cabbage

LOW INTERTIDAL ZONE

(90 per cent underwater)

Giant green sea anemone

Purple sea urchin

Pink coralline algae

Kelp

Its mottled coloring making it practically invisible on the sand, a ghost crab scuttles along the beach just above the high-tide line. Despite its penchant for dry land, this four-inch-wide creature must return regularly to the surf in order to moisten its gills.

An extraordinary aspect of the barnacle's adaptation is revealed when it first settles on its bit of rock. The search for a place to settle down is accomplished when it is a tiny, vulnerable larval creature called a cypris, swimming among the plankton after being discharged from the parental shell upon hatching.

The cypris has six pairs of legs, two delicate shells and the rudiments of an eye. When a cypris is swept onto a rock face in a wave, modified suckers on its antennae enable it to hold on to the hard surface. Secured in a head-down position, the barnacle will never move again during its lifetime of from three to five years.

After finding its permanent home, the barnacle begins the business of getting itself anatomically reorganized for adulthood and forming the shell that will protect it from the sun, the sea and predatory animals. The shell is a truncated cone composed of half a dozen plates, topped by a four-plated valve. The valve can be closed when the tide recedes, to hold in moisture and keep out sunlight and predators, and opened for food-gathering when the tide is in. To feed, the barnacle extends its legs through the opened valve, fanning them in the tidewater to comb out food particles, then draws them inside so the food can be devoured. This graceful process is repeated every few seconds when the creature is submerged in salt water.

The most striking aspect of a barnacle colony is its density. One census of a 1,000-yard stretch of rocky shore produced an estimate of a billion barnacles in residence, plus the estimate that each of the hermaphroditic creatures would produce an average of 1,000 larvae in a year's time. That is a million adult barnacles and a billion larvae per linear yard of beach. Procreation on a grand scale clearly ranks high as a means of ensuring the species' survival in its harsh environment.

Barnacles are often joined by periwinkles and limpets in the high intertidal zone. Limpets are well adapted to withstand the pounding of heavy surf: Their conical shells break the impact of the waves, and their broad feet grip the rocks and keep them from being swept away. The secret of the limpet's strong grip is a combination of suction and a sticky mucus. An especially fascinating feature of limpets is that the shape of their shell varies according to the violence of the surf at their particular site. The difference can be seen when limpets living on opposite sides of the same rock are compared. The limpets on the exposed side will have taller shells with narrower bases, better for deflecting the fierce waves. On the sheltered side, or in rock pools where the wave action is gentle or nearly nonexistent, the shell is broader and flatter.

Brown seaweeds, so colored because their bright green chlorophyll is darkened by other pigments, appear just below the barnacles. Their rather sparse and stunted growth reflects the difficult conditions of life high on the shore. Desiccation is the great danger for them here, and the fronds are small—no more than about seven inches—so that they expose minimal surface area to the drying air. (Lower down or on a sheltered rocky coast, a similar species of the same genus may grow to be seven feet long.) Although it may become black and crisp under a hot summer sun, the seaweed usually does not dry out altogether, and its suppleness is quickly restored when the tide does wash over it. Seaweed contends with the other problem of life on an exposed rock face—the pounding of the surf, which threatens to sweep it away—by gripping the rocks with flattened-out, finger-like extensions of its fronds, called holdfasts.

The middle intertidal zone is the band of shore that is completely covered and uncovered each day. In the purest sense, it is the true intertidal zone, for the parts of the shore above it and below it are not so regularly exposed and submerged. The inhabitants here, unlike those higher up on the shore,

Barnacles extend feathery legs through the tops of their tepee-shaped shells to strain tiny particles of food from the tidewater. When the tide ebbs, the barnacles retreat into their shells, fortifying themselves against both dehydration and predators.

are not semiterrestrial but are fundamentally dependent on the sea. Yet these forms of life differ from true marine plants and animals in being able to endure some exposure to air.

This zone bristles with clusters of blue-black mussels, each one anchored tightly to the rocks by the byssus, a silky black thread spun out by the mussel when it first gains a foothold on a solid surface. So dense is the blanket of mussels that it seems like a rocky surface itself rather than an assemblage of individual living creatures. Interspersed among the mussel beds, there may be colonies of ivory-shelled goose barnacles, whose tough but flexible stalks enable them to yield gracefully to the direction of the surf.

Below the normal low-tide line is a band of shore that is uncovered only occasionally, by the lowest tide of the month or year. Many of the organisms living here qualify as true creatures of the sea, since they are able to endure only the briefest and rarest exposure to air; but such authentically intertidal creatures as littorines and kelp share the space. The low intertidal is, in fact, more abundantly endowed with life than any of the zones above it. The leathery brown Laminaria, often known as kelp, oarweed or sea tangles, are the dominant plants, growing so luxuriantly that they form veritable forests at the edge of the sea. Their broad fronds support a wealth of tiny animals, among them delicately tentacled creatures that live in colonies called sea lace. Beneath the tangles of kelp may be found soft, thick mats of yellow-green sponges, and these shelter other little creatures: threadlike sea worms, miniature kelp crabs, glistening sea squirts or tiny brittle stars.

The rocky floor of this lowest tidal zone is often encrusted with the delicate pink corallines—algae that, despite their resemblance to corals, are plants that cope with the action of the waves by encasing themselves in limy skeletons. Especially where there are cracks or crevices in the rocks, chrysanthemum-like sea anemones extend their graceful, sometimes iridescent tentacles to gather food when the tide is in. Their relatives, the feathery, plantlike hydroids, may attach themselves to the fronds of seaweeds, to rocks or to the shells of mussels. Spiny sea urchins anchor themselves to the rocks or nestle against the soft bodies of sponges. Crabs and other crustaceans scuttle about, and when the tide is in, fish venture in from farther out to sea.

Strewn like blossoms over the rocks and seaweed at low tide are sea stars, which display a wide array of colors—blood red, purple, peach, blue, gray or cream. The brilliance of their hues and the symmetry of their multiarmed bodies may easily distract an observer from considering their lethal efficiency in preying on shellfish.

In a hundred other ways, this band of the shore is a lively scene of competition and conflict. The cozy manner in which a sea squirt nestles against a sponge belies the fact that the little creature is engaged in a determined attempt to dislodge the sponge from its precious bit of space, a struggle that will doom the loser. The flowery anemone is a deadly enemy of the mussel, and colonies of anemones are often seen surrounded by all that remains of their hapless prey, a litter of blue-black shells. The delicate hydroid fires a shower of poisonous, stinging cells at any worm or small crustacean that ventures within the grasp of its undulating tentacles, which then convey the paralyzed animal to the hydroid's mouth. Sea ur-

Its ridge-line record of seaward growth clearly visible in this aerial view, Cape Krusenstern sweeps out into the Chukchi Sea, enclosing marshy Krusenstern Lagoon. Changing storm patterns during the cape's 5,000-year history explain the varied orientations of the ridges.

A Coastal Tale of Time

At Cape Krusenstern, on Alaska's northwest coast, freak storms and geological happenstance have turned the usual record of past events on its side. The cape's 114 parallel ridges—each one a former coastline—form a horizontal sequence as neatly indexed for age as the vertically layered soils or sediments in which evidence of the past is usually preserved.

Arching out to sea in a furrowed swath about two miles wide and eight miles long, the tundra-covered ridges resemble "a great garden that has for some seasons lain fallow," in the words of archeologist J. Louis Giddings. But the plow that shaped the six-to-eight-foot-high embankments was meteorological. Every 50 to 75 years, in a process that continues today, waves from a rare southwesterly storm attack vast offshore gravel banks and heap sediment on shore, forming a new coastal ridge.

Spanning 5,000 years, the sequence of ridges preserves tools, bones, and ruined shelters from ancient Eskimo cultures. The result is "an unequaled archeological sequence," in Giddings' words, that moves step by step from ancient remains on the inland ridges to more recent artifacts near the shore.

chins ravage kelp. Yet a human observer can hardly detect all this warfare; conducted in silence and with a minimum of visible motion, it presents a frozen tableau to our eyes.

Similarly, a pristine expanse of sandy beach may seem to be barren of life. The uppermost part of the beach is indeed quite hostile to most creatures. Here, well beyond the highest high-tide mark, no cool wash of tidal water, or even spray, reaches the sand to refresh it. But where the sand is intermittently wet by the tides, the lifeless face of the beach conceals a busy lilliputian world beneath the surface. Because of capillary attraction, each grain of sand retains around it a film of water. Through the subsurface liquid, millions of microscopic creatures can move: unicelled animals and plants; microscopic juveniles of slightly larger animals; water mites; tiny shrimplike creatures; and minute flatworms.

The universe within the sand of open coast beaches is also inhabited by larger creatures. Very few of these animals can be seen on the surface; it is too shifting and unstable, incessantly being rearranged by the surf. But the evidence of their presence is everywhere. The wet sand of more protected shores is marked by the thin tracks of burrowing clams, by groves of tiny protruding tubes erected by exotic plumed worms, and by hundreds of little holes perforating the surface—the openings of the tiny burrows of ghost shrimp.

Under their blanket of sand, the beach creatures are protected from the onslaught of the waves, from the drying rays of the sun and from the devastation of frost and ice. Their secret habitats, tiny burrows and holes in the sand away from the variable and unpredictable conditions at the surface, contrast sharply with the distinctive bands of life that are so prominent on rocky shores. An underground existence poses some problems, however—most important, how to move and how to eat under a smothering mass of wet sand.

The two most common soft-bodied inhabitants of the beach, annelid worms and bivalve mollusks, both solve the problem of how to dig down into the sand in the same way: They change the shape of their bodies and alternately push and pull their way through the sand. A worm leads with its head; a bivalve, such as a clam, with its foot.

A close-up view of the locomotion of a razorshell clam (which is all but impossible, for once the animal is exposed or senses the presence of an intruder, it closes its shell instantly) would reveal the downward prowling of the pulpy foot of this delicately elongated bivalve. While probing, the razorshell's foot is slender and somewhat pointed, but when fully extended it dilates, anchoring itself and drawing the rest of the clam after it. At the same time, the razorshell contracts its shells, emitting a squirt of water that loosens the sand just ahead of the foot. The creature's streamlined shape facilitates its progress and helps to account for the astonishing speed with which it can dig into sand—as it does the instant it is exposed by the receding tide.

The presence of lugworms is somewhat more obvious. These creatures abound on many protected North American and European beaches and tide flats. The location of each animal is pinpointed by the presence on the beach of a tiny crater, perhaps an inch deep, and a nearby cone of sand about four inches from the crater. The worm lies within the sand, cozily tucked

TEEMING TENANTS OF THE BEACH

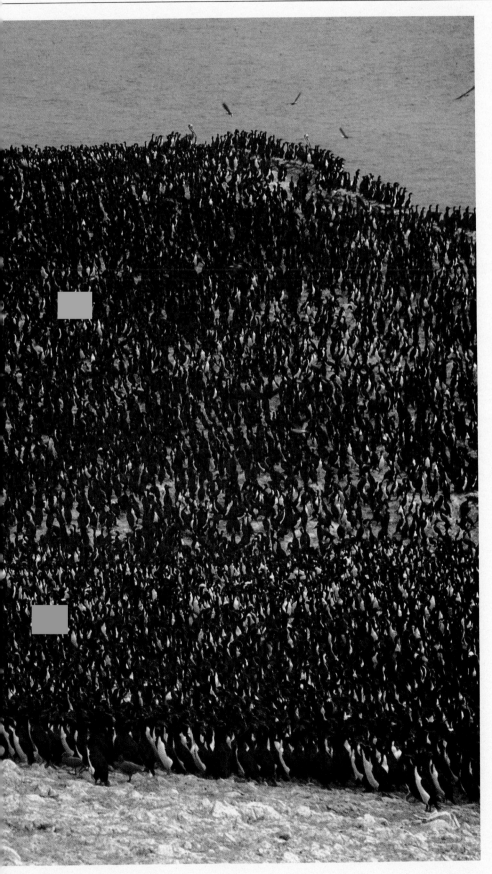

As befits disputed ground between land and sea, the shore is frequented by creatures with divided allegiances. They depend on the rich life of the sea for nourishment but, because they belong to classes that are basically terrestrial, return to the shore to rest and breed.

Many sea birds, the most visible of shore denizens, limit their contact with the sea to forays for food. Cormorants, though superlative fishers, must allow their wings to dry in the sun after each venture. Sanderlings, the most gingerly of shore birds, barely wet their long legs as they pluck morsels of food from the swash that advances up the beach with each breaking wave.

Seals, sea lions and walruses—seagoing mammals that spend much of their time on shore—seem more at home in the water than on land. Ashore, the flippers and layer of insulating blubber that are essential to their marine existence make them clumsy and slow. Except for the territorial battles of the breeding season, their time on land is spent mostly in rest and sunbathing.

Streamlined sea turtles, which have flippers and lungs that are specialized for long dives, are perhaps the most completely marine of the seagoing creatures that maintain ties to dry land. They begin their lives on sandy beaches, but the vulnerable hatchlings quickly escape to the open sea. Only after years of watery roaming do the females return to shore, for a few hours, to lay their eggs.

On a small island south of Pisco, Peru, cormorants mass on ground whitened by their accumulated droppings. Heavy-boned and capable of squeezing the trapped air from their bodies and plumage, cormorants can dive to depths of 70 feet in search of fish.

Fleet-footed sanderlings forage on wet sand, narrowly avoiding the receding swash. As each wave withdraws, the birds sprint down the beach to snatch up tiny sea creatures swept ashore by the surf before the prey have a chance to burrow their way into the sand.

Replete after feeding, bull walruses loll on a sunny beach on Round Island, Alaska. To reach the clams, sea snails, and other shellfish that are its staple foods, a walrus can dive 200 feet to the sea floor, where it rakes the bottom with its tusks to uproot its catch.

Sandwich terns nest among dune grasses near the entrance to the Arcachon Basin, a bay in southern France. These slender, narrow-winged members of the gull family spot shrimp, squid, and fish while hovering far above the waves, then plunge seaward to snag a meal.

Marine iguanas scuttle into the water of the Galápagos Islands. The world's only seagoing species of lizard, iguanas use their powerful, narrow tails to propel themselves out to sea-washed rocks, where they feed on seaweed.

Her laborious landward progress clearly tracked in the sand, a leatherback turtle carefully buries her clutch of eggs. The leatherback, which may reach a length of seven feet and a weight of 1,200 pounds, lives in the ocean and comes ashore only for breeding.

into a U-shaped tunnel. Its head lies under the crater, its tail under the cone. Like all marine worms characteristic of sandy beaches, lugworms cope with the problem of obtaining food while buried in sand by simply ingesting the sand itself. The worm digests the organic particles in the sand, such as bacteria or animal remains, and expels the inorganic remainder. As it takes in sand, the funnel-shaped depression is hollowed out above its mouth, and as the worm expels its castings, they build up into the little conical mound at the other end. Where lugworms abound, they keep the amount of decaying organic matter on the beach in proper balance. In one year, the lugworm population of an acre of beach can process nearly 2,000 tons of sand.

Not all of the burrowing animals of the sandy or muddy shore can take in sand or mud. Mollusks, such as the razorshells, soft-shell clams and cockles, extract their food from sea water. Razorshells and soft-shell clams, for example, are equipped with siphons, which they push up through the sand to inhale swirling sea water. As the incoming water passes through the animal's gills, large particles such as grains of sand are filtered out and expelled through the siphon. The finest particles, which include minute planktonic animals and plants, pass through to be digested.

Only a few creatures can endure the attacking waves and the shifting sand of the beach surface. One of them is the mole crab, a hardy creature that thrives in this surf-swept world by exploiting the fresh supplies of food brought in from the sea by the waves. This little crustacean is indeed mole-like, with its short, pawlike legs and its tiny, nearly blind eyes. In order to feed, the mole crab digs backward into the sand by whirling its tail appendages until only its plumelike, fringed antennae and mouth are above the surface. Facing the ocean, the crab waits for the surf to roll in. When it comes, the mole crab waits until a wave's energy is spent and the water is streaming back to the sea. Suddenly, the mole crab—indeed mole crabs by the hundreds, for they dwell in colonies and all feed at the same moment—thrusts its antennae up into the receding wave. The appendages are so finely feathered and so dense that they enmesh hundreds of microscopic plants and animals from the foaming surf and shifting sand. After trapping its food, the crab quickly picks over its antennae with its mouth appendages, and digs in to await the next wave. The crabs migrate up and down on the beach with the ebb and flow of the tide, always maintaining their special place at the edge of the surf.

Higher on the beach, beyond the reach of all the waves except the highest waves of the highest tides, is a zone that, like the uppermost zone of the rocky shore, belongs neither completely to the land nor completely to the sea. The few animals that inhabit these dry sands at the top of the beach would appear to be terrestrial intruders on the shore. But their way of life reflects their marine origin and continuing link to the sea. The ghost crab, for example, often digs its burrow at the foot of the dunes, as one might expect a true land dweller to do. But this habit is misleading, for the ghost crab is not an air breather. It begins its life in the sea and, as an adult, must return to it several times each day to wet its gills. When it does so, its ambiguous relationship with the sea is apparent. Rather than submerging, the ghost crab stations itself just beyond the reach of most of the breaking waves. It stands sideways in the sand, bracing itself with the legs on its landward side and waiting for a wave higher than most to arrive. When the wave comes, the ghost crab is drenched for a brief moment, enough to refill a bronchial chamber that encloses its gills. Then it hurries back up the beach to dry land.

Like the ghost crab, the beach flea, or sand hopper, may be poised at a dramatic moment in its evolution. It seems to be on the verge of making a clean break with the sea and becoming a true terrestrial creature. It has gotten as far as the high beach and never enters the water of its own accord, but it can usually swim well enough to escape all but the strongest waves. Still, the beach flea depends on the sea for its sustenance, feeding on the remains of fish and crabs or on fragments of marine plants such as sea lettuce, eelgrass or kelp that are left behind on the beach in the wake of the receding tide.

This tiny creature establishes its home for a day at a time at the top of the beach, above the high-tide line, and digs into the sand with ferocious energy. Within 10 minutes it excavates a tunnel about six inches deep—comparable to a person digging a hole 60 feet deep with hands only in the same period of time. Once the beach flea has dug to the requisite depth, it carefully closes the "door" behind it by stuffing the hole with sand grains. The occupied burrow thus cannot easily be detected at the surface; the holes visible on the upper beach are the entrances of deserted burrows. Snug in its refuge, the beach flea waits for the tide to recede and for darkness to fall. (No one knows how it senses the latter condition, for surely no light can penetrate down into the deep reaches of the burrow.) But somehow the beach flea knows when it may come out to feed, safe from the menacing shore birds that peruse the beach during the daylight hours, and assured of a rich supply of food at the tide's edge. Ω

Fronds of giant kelp stream in the tidal current off Gaviota, California. Supple but firmly anchored to the rocky bottom, the seaweed flourishes in the strong waves and currents of water 60 to 90 feet deep along the Pacific coast of North America.

LIFE BETWEEN THE TIDES

Alternately pounded by waves and bared to extremes of weather, a tide-washed rocky coast is hostile both to terrestrial life and to creatures of the open sea. Yet hundreds of species of plants and animals have developed the means to thrive on this surface.

At each level of the shore, different stresses reign supreme in the lives of intertidal creatures. In the high splash zone, where weeks may pass between the storms that dampen the rock, a few marine life-forms have evolved the capacity to feed and breathe on land. They also endure conditions that are deadly to other sea creatures: the ultraviolet rays in sunlight, the drying effect of the open air, and the temperature extremes of summer sun and winter storms.

Farther down the shore, where the tide rolls in daily, intertidal marine creatures can rely on the sea for oxygen and nourishment. But they must attune their lives to the rhythm of the tides, surrendering to hours-long dormancy when the tide recedes. And they face other stresses. Wave action is fiercest here, and it continually tests each creature's toughness and hold on the rock face.

The middle and lower reaches of the shore host a more plentiful and varied population of intertidal creatures than the top of the shoreface. Here, the dangers of a hostile environment are compounded by competition for space and nourishment and the ravages of predators. The fact that the tidal pools abound with life, and that the shoreface is layered with other communities of differing densities and compositions all the way up to the scattered pioneers of the splash zone, testifies to the infinite inventiveness of nature.

Behind a curtain of kelp fronds, the exuberant life of the lower intertidal region at Tatoosh Island, Washington, daubs the floor of the sea with color. Pincushion-like sea urchins and tentacled sea anemones share a rock surface that is encrusted with pink coralline algae.

The High, Dry Intertidal Fringe

The sparse life of the upper shore—dampened only by the spray from the highest breakers—is almost completely liberated from its marine origins. For example, sea slaters (relatives of shrimps and crabs) and littorine snails have forsaken the sea so thoroughly that they breathe air and may drown if they are immersed for long.

But these creatures of the splash zone are still dependent on the sea's rare returns to the top of the shore, for neither has outgrown a marine animal's need for constant moisture. During dry spells that may last for weeks, littorine snails seal their shells with tiny trap doors and enter a kind of suspended animation, while sea slaters seek refuge in damp crevices.

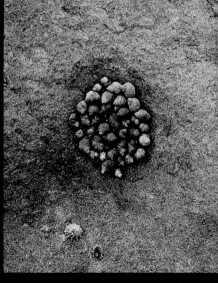

Littorine snails reduce their moisture loss during a dry spell on the upper shore by clustering in a hollow on the rock face. When spray or very high tides moisten the rock, the half-inch-long snails forage for algae, which they harvest with rasplike scrapers.

In uncharacteristic surroundings, an inch-long sea slater crosses a luxuriant patch of seaweed. Sea slaters are usually found well above the region of abundant plant growth, where they survive on the scraps of seaweed that are washed within their reach by high surf.

Between the green seaweeds at high-tide mark and the mosses at the edge of the forest on Waadah Island, Washington, lies the highest intertidal region, where rocks are stained dark with algal growth. Littorine snails

A Crowded Midshore Community

At the middle level of the shore, which is washed regularly by tidewater, the lives of the myriad creatures that encrust the shoreface are shaped not only by their wave-battered environment but also by a web of interactions. Predators are a major force at this level, where marauding whelks scourge colonies of barnacles and mussels. And competition for space is rife; one barnacle species crowds out individuals of another species that attach themselves nearby.

But coexistence benefits some intertidal creatures. Snails escape the brunt of the waves and, at ebb tide, the threat of dehydration by sheltering among seaweed fronds. And the hermit crab, a tide-pool scavenger, depends even more on other organisms for shelter, housing itself in cast-off snail shells.

The carnivorous snails called whelks feed on a cluster of mussels by first drilling into the shells of their prey with rasping mouth parts and shell-softening secretions. The whelks then suck out the flesh, leaving empty mussel shells marked with telltale boreholes.

Housed in the shell of a dead whelk, a hermit crab picks its way across a sponge, beneath the overhanging fringe of an anemone's tentacles. The crabs are so finely matched to their borrowed homes that their bodies have evolved a rightward twist to fit the spiral of snail shells.

Littorine snails cling to rockweed splayed on the rock face by the outgoing tide. The seaweed provides both food and shelter, and some snail species lay their eggs among the fronds.

Two barnacle species share a rock face: a larger one with a fluted shell, and a smaller brown-shelled species. If the larger barnacles become more numerous, they will crush and slowly pry loose their less robust relatives.

Competition for space and food is intense in the thickly populated middle and lower reaches of the shore. But many intertidal organisms have evolved traits that protect them from the struggle.

An example of the luxuriant plant growth of this region is the sea palm, a seaweed found on the Pacific coast of North America. Its resilient stalk and tenacious base enable it to withstand waves that would shred or sweep away many other seaweed species, which typi- cally colonize more sheltered shores.

Two animal inhabitants of the middle and lower zones, the sea spider and the striped chiton, elude competition through their adaptation to a single food source. The chiton thrives on coralline algae, a plant spurned by other intertidal vegetarians, while the sea spider is one of the few creatures capable of dining on sea anemones. Presumably, the spider is protected from the stinging tentacles by its thick exoskeleton.

A sea spider prowls the jelly-like surface of a tunicate, an amorphous animal resembling a marine sponge. Half-inch-long sea spiders, unrelated to land spiders, rarely stray from the sea anemones on which they feed.

Beneath its shield of eight articulated shell plates, a striped chiton grazes in a patch of coralline algae. The two-inch mollusk is so dependent on its single food that the free- swimming chiton larvae can metamorphose into adults only if the algae are nearby.

Sea palms cling to a rocky shore whitened by barnacles. Heavy surf flattens the 18-inch seaweed against the rocks, but when the waves withdraw, the plants right themselves.

A Tide-washed Garden at the Base of the Shore

For all their resemblance to flowers in an undersea garden, the most striking and colorful creatures of the lower intertidal realm are animals. Many are sedentary; others are capable of slow, gliding motion. But most have familiar body parts such as mouths and digestive cavities, as well as the sensitivity to their surroundings essential to survival in a world full of dangers. In addition, most lower intertidal animals are superbly adapted to defending themselves, with jaws or stings, or to warding off attack, with shells, spines or unpalatability.

Some animals of this realm, despite their grace and apparent innocence, are rapacious predators. Many starfish use the powerful suction of their numerous tiny feet to pry open shellfish and reach the flesh inside, while the colorful tentacles of sea anemones can prove a deadly trap for small sea creatures.

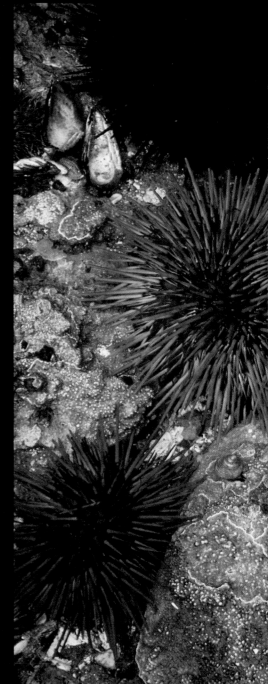

A serpulid tube worm displays plumelike tentacles that strain floating food particles from the water. When eyespots at the base of the tentacles detect a shadow, the worm retreats into its coiled, limy tube, stoppering the entrance with the trumpet-shaped structure that is visible behind the plumes.

A blood star, a tide-pool scavenger, ornaments branching coralline algae. Like its predatory relatives, the blood star locates its food through nerve endings that are sensitive to chemical traces, then edges toward it by rhythmically extending and retracting the hundreds of tiny tube-shaped feet on its underside.

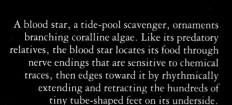

Two species of sea urchin bristle in shades of
red and purple. The creature's phalanx of spines
discourages attackers and also traps the
urchin's staple food—floating scraps of seaweed.

A graceful, opalescent nudibranch, perched on
twiglike coralline algae, is the marine equivalent
of the common land slug. These inch-long
shell-less snails, seemingly defenseless, exude an
acid mucus that is unpalatable to predators.

Like eerie sunflowers, six-inch-wide sea anemones carpet the lowest reaches of a rocky shore. Small animals that venture too near are paralyzed by tiny

poison darts on the anemone's tentacles, then are swept into the central, gaping mouth.

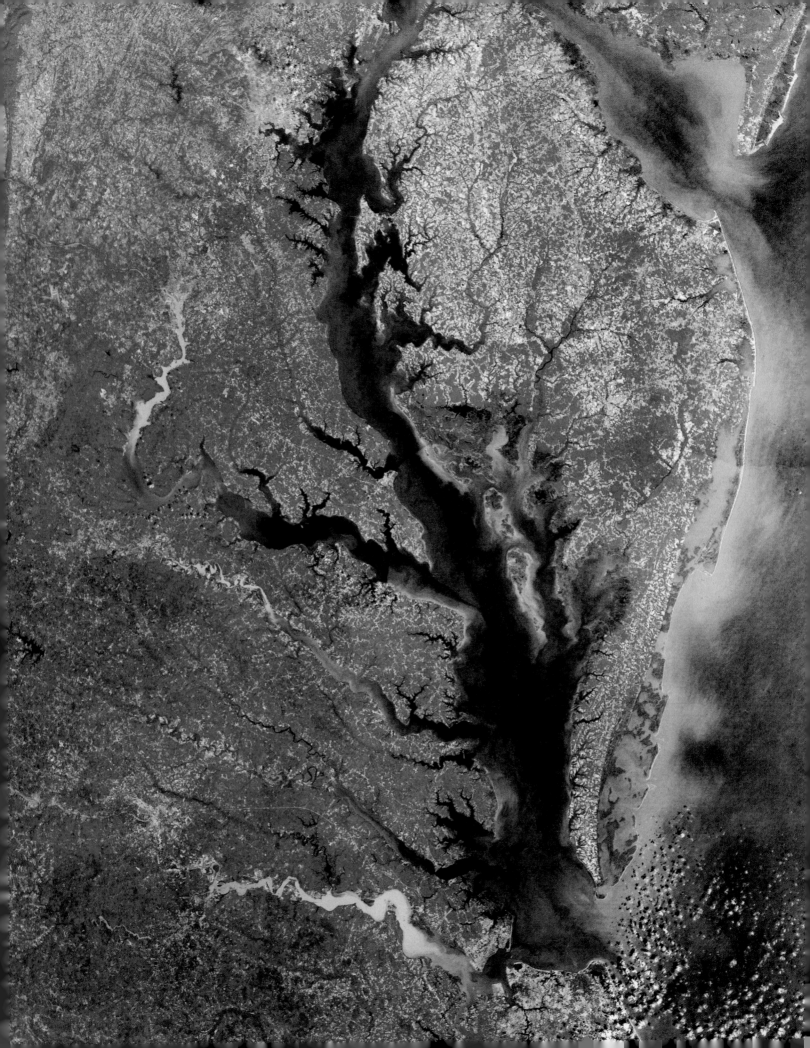

Chapter 3

A FECUND REALM

Along the Eastern Seaboard of the United States, spring has taken hold with its usual flourish. Flowers cast their scent on the air, and the trees are leafed out. But the change of seasons has not reached to the murky depths of the Chesapeake Bay. Clouded by the sediment deposits of more than 20 major rivers, continuously shifted and stirred by salt-water tides contesting with fresh-water runoff, the waters of the Bay resist the increasing strength of the sun; light that reaches depths of 300 feet in the open ocean manages a penetration of less than a foot here when the runoff is strong, and water temperatures change slowly.

Sometime during the second or third week of May, however, a subtle signal finally reaches the floor of the Bay—an incremental warming, perhaps, or a hint of changing salt content. Its nature is not fully comprehended by science; but to the organisms whose senses are attuned to it, the signal is a clarion call. The response begins with a random stirring that, if it could be seen in the gloom, might be mistaken for a shifting of the muddy floor itself. Then, first by the score, then in hundreds and soon in untold thousands, there emerge from the mud a multitude of singular creatures.

Their hard-shelled bodies resemble two saucers, joined at the edges and colored a dark blue-green, with highlights of blue and pearly cream. Two eye stalks protrude from the forward edge, and ten legs are joined to the side and back edges. As the creatures awake from their winter-long dormancy, they flex the heavily muscled claws of the foremost pair of legs, clamber out of their silty blanket, and skitter over the mud with their six walking legs. Or they loft themselves into the water to swim with remarkable speed and agility, propelled by two flexible swimming legs that have paddle-shaped ends. They are blue crabs, whose formal name, *Callinectes sapidus,* is a combination of Greek and Latin that translates as "beautiful and tasty swimmer."

Shortly after awaking and beginning their purposeful, swarming migration up from the depths of the Bay, the crabs are overtaken by what might appear to be seizures. They jerk and twirl, then they swell dramatically, splitting their tough armor; eventually the organisms struggle free of their own external skeletons. For hours or even days, the soft, vulnerable creatures lie near their former shells, gulping water to expand their cramped and wrinkled body tissue, gradually recovering from the exhaustion of their recent struggle. Then, with their new and larger shells hardening in place, they resume their urgent journey. They spread out to favored

Maryland and Virginia, their vegetation crimson in this infrared satellite image, bracket the Chesapeake Bay, the largest estuary in the continental United States. The sediment in some of the rivers that supply the Chesapeake with fresh water appears as bright blue.

summer haunts in the shallows, migrating up the great rivers, winding creeks and sheltered coves that open into the Bay, seeking out the thick stands of waving eelgrass where they will find the carrion that is their principal food.

This teeming migration of the deep is mimicked on the surface of the water by fleets of workboats that take to the shallows to gather up the arriving blue crabs. Most of the Virginians and Marylanders who make their living from the waters of the Chesapeake have been absent in recent weeks; in late April and early May, after the end of the oyster season and before the first run of the blue crabs, they repair their equipment and perform other onshore tasks. But now the continuing labor of harvesting the bounty of the Bay resumes, the men working into the night, women and children working shifts, all driving themselves to exhaustion to reap the sudden abundance.

For 300 years the Chesapeake has sustained successive generations of crabbers, oystermen and fishermen, descendants of the insular and individualistic colonists who settled the shores and islands of the Bay in the 17th and 18th Centuries. The 18,000 or so full-time watermen who wrest their livelihood from the Bay today do so with tools that have advanced little since those early times. Crabbers still employ the ancestral methods of setting out cagelike traps, called crab pots, or running trotlines—strands of cotton up to a mile long, baited every three feet or so with pickled eel. The trotline is laid in promising shallows, usually near thick stands of eelgrass, and hauled up at intervals. The crabs attempting to make a meal of the bait refuse to release their powerful grip even when hauled clear of the water. Many oystermen employ a backbreaking procedure called tonging, in which they scoop their prey from the bottom by hand with metal tongs on long wooden shafts.

The dependence of the Chesapeake crab and oyster industries on manual operations and preindustrial technology would seem to imply a modest-sized harvest at best. That is not the case. So fertile is the Bay that in an average year it yields about 65 million pounds of blue crabs, a considerable portion of the total U.S. catch of more than a quarter of a billion pounds. The Chesapeake's annual oyster production is often worth more than $20 million (one fourth of the U.S. catch); the Bay yields more than half the national catch of steamer clams and leads the country in production of several varieties of fish—notably the striped bass, or rockfish. The Bay's productivity is not limited to its physical boundaries; a sizable proportion of the fish that populate the open Atlantic coastal waters of North America—possibly 70 per cent—are spawned or spend a critical part of their lives in the Chesapeake.

This immense, fecund cornucopia of life is an estuary—a protected arm of the sea into which rivers continuously pour fresh water, creating a blend of tide, current and changing salinity unlike that of any other environment in the world. The Chesapeake sprawls for 200 miles from the northeastern corner of Maryland southward to the Virginia capes off Norfolk. With nearly 1.5 million acres of water and 4,000 miles of undulating shoreline, it is by far the largest estuary in the United States and is among the most splendid in the world.

Estuaries figure large in human history, and not just as food sources. Their sheltered waters usually make excellent harbors, and many estuaries

A spit made from riverborne sediments and shaped by longshore ocean currents shelters the mouth of the Klamath River in northern California, creating a small but classic estuary.

are fed by navigable rivers that afford transportation routes to inland agricultural, trading and trapping areas. (As a bonus, oceangoing mariners found that anchoring in the fresh waters at the upper end of an estuary could kill several months' accumulation of barnacles on a ship's hull.) London, Hong Kong, Calcutta and New York are just a few of the great ports that are sited on estuaries.

Neither a river nor a sea, an estuary is something in between; it is a body of water whose geography gives it some protection from the rigors of wind and wave and whose composition is an ever-shifting mix of fresh water from continental rivers and salt water from ocean tides. Many bays are estuaries—Ireland's Galway and Donegal, Australia's Port Phillip, and America's San Francisco, Galveston and Delaware Bays, for instance. But not all estuaries are bays. The roll call of estuaries includes many inlets and sounds, the famous firths of Scotland, nearly all of the fjords of Scandinavia, and the seaward extremities of some of the great river deltas, such as the Nile and the Mississippi.

This diversity of character is accounted for by variations in such things as mode of origin, rate of sediment accumulation, and relative strength of the rivers and the tides. The most common type of estuary is the drowned river valley, of which the Chesapeake Bay is a prime example. The Bay's original channel, still traceable in its middle depths, was that of the Susquehanna River, the longest waterway on the Eastern Seaboard of the United States. A shallow, swift river that rises in the worn-down Appalachian Mountains of upstate New York, the Susquehanna eases across the rich plains of eastern Pennsylvania's Piedmont plateau, and once flowed southward through what

A French Landmark in a Quagmire

The natural and inevitable death of an estuary in western France has put geological processes on a collision course with esthetics. The focus of this singular conflict is the magnificent medieval church that crowns a tiny granite island in the eastern end of Normandy's Bay of St.-Michel. Until recently, high tides regularly surrounded Mont-St.-Michel with water, imposing on it a splendid, if temporary, isolation from the mainland—and giving it a special appeal that has drawn religious and architectural pilgrims to the site for a millennium.

But estuaries themselves are by nature temporary. The Bay of St.-Michel was formed less than 10,000 years ago, as melting Ice Age glaciers caused the sea level to rise and invade the French coastline. Since then, rivers emptying into the bay have laid down about 50 feet of sediment on its floor and have continuously extended the shoreline, shrinking the bay and reducing the distance between the church and the mainland to less than a mile. Parts of the extensive mud flats that were once inundated by the tides are now high and dry enough to support spreading vegetation.

Human activities have sped the process. The draining of the bay's flanking marshes for agriculture and the damming and diking of its tributary rivers for flood control have accelerated the build-up of the land and diminished the scouring effect of the streams. By 1980, only one high tide in 10 could extend its waters far enough across the accumulated silt to transform Mont-St.-Michel into an island.

The age-old contrast between the watery isolation of France's Mont-St.-Michel at high tide (*left*) and the surrounding mud flats at low tide (*inset*) has been diminished by the proximity of a grassy finger of land that extends from the Normandy mainland. The earthen causeway constructed a century ago helped sediment build above the water line.

Modeling the Defense of Mont-St.-Michel

The continuing siltation around Mont-St.-Michel finally prompted the French Ministry of the Environment to organize a comprehensive investigation of ways to keep the site from becoming land-locked. Scientists undertook a battery of studies: They assessed the force of the rivers entering the estuary, for instance, and marked the silt with fluorescent and radioactive tracers to follow its movements. At the Central Laboratory for Hydraulics of France, a scale model of the 38 square miles of mud flats surrounding Mont-St.-Michel was built to test the effects on sedimentation of removing or modifying dams and dikes.

The results were encouraging. Scientists concluded that with quick action, the scouring force of the rivers and tides could be increased and sedimentation slowed down, preserving the marine character of this coastal treasure.

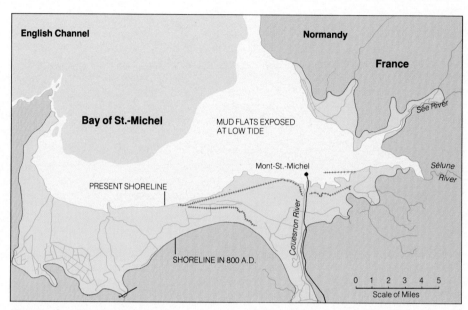

English Channel

Normandy

France

Bay of St.-Michel

MUD FLATS EXPOSED AT LOW TIDE

Sée River

Mont-St.-Michel

Sélune River

PRESENT SHORELINE

Couesnon River

SHORELINE IN 800 A.D.

0 1 2 3 4 5
Scale of Miles

The map above illustrates the three-mile advance of the shoreline toward Mont-St.-Michel over the course of 12 centuries. Drainage channels (*blue*) and dikes (*red*) have contributed to the filling-in of the bay.

A scale model of Mont-St.-Michel simulates conditions at low tide. For this test, one portion of the earthen causeway has been replaced with a pile-supported roadway that allows water to circulate more freely.

is now Maryland and Virginia, almost to the North Carolina border, before it met the Atlantic.

With the end of the last ice age some 12,000 years ago, the melting ice sheets began to swell the world's oceans. The Atlantic advanced back up the continental shelf, pushed through the gap between the promontories now known as Cape Charles and Cape Henry about 10,000 years ago and eventually inundated the Susquehanna valley and the lower reaches of several smaller rivers that would later bear a marvelous mélange of English and American Indian names: Rappahannock, York, James, Severn, Potomac, Patuxent.

The Chesapeake had gained its present majestic proportions by about 3,000 years ago, its indented profile a reminder of the ancient river systems far beneath its waves. Other estuaries that were formed in the same way but along rivers with fewer tributaries, such as the Hudson and the St. Lawrence, took on far less complex shapes.

The rivers that pour their volumes of fresh water into estuaries are, to varying degrees, laden with sediment from the interior of the continents. In areas where the tides and offshore currents are strong, the sediment is carried out to sea or transported along the shore. But if the sediment load of the river is so great that it overpowers the effect of the tides, the material settles in and eventually fills the estuary.

Where a sizable, sediment-loaded river empties into a protected body of water that has a narrow tidal range, as is the case at the mouth of the Mississippi, the result is usually the formation of a delta—a triangular accumulation of silt that breaks the river's flow into a myriad of branching channels. India's Ganges and Brahmaputra Rivers, which meet the ocean at the head of the Bay of Bengal, carry about 700 million tons of sediment each year—more than twice the content of the Mississippi. A vast delta has formed as a result, despite a large tidal range and extensive wave action.

Because of their low elevation, deltas are frequently flooded by storm-swollen rivers, which distribute fresh supplies of rich soil and make the deltas regions of great fertility. Many early agricultural societies—the Egyptian and Sumerian civilizations, to mention two prominent examples —flourished on river deltas.

Another kind of estuary is found sandwiched between coastal barrier islands and the shore of the mainland; this is the bar-built estuary, or lagoon, examples of which are the Vadehavet tidal area of Denmark and the Waddenzee of the Netherlands. Such estuaries are usually shallow, because barrier islands tend to form in waters just a few yards deep, where waves and currents deposit sediment in long ridges. Unlike drowned river valleys, lagoons are not at the mouths of rivers and do not receive significant freshwater runoff; often they are fed only by small streams. In addition, the inlets that punctuate the islands and allow tidal currents to flow into the lagoons are too narrow and restrictive to permit the sudden enormous influxes of salt water from the open sea that characterize other estuaries. Large waves and strong currents are rare; most lagoons are quiet bodies of water, ruffled only gently by the wind.

Bar-built estuaries are found along 80 to 90 per cent of the Atlantic and Gulf coasts of the United States, but along only 10 to 20 per cent of the Pacific coast, where the continental shelf is too narrow and steep to allow barrier islands to form. Another reason for the scarcity of estuaries is that few rivers reach the sea through the great chains of mountains that separate the Pacific coast from the interior, and those few are limited in their flow, since the land behind the mountain chains is generally arid. However, the same tectonic episodes that thrust up the Pacific mountain chains caused portions of the California coast to drop, transforming their river valleys into large estuarine systems. San Francisco Bay and the Juan de Fuca Strait are examples of these tectonic estuaries.

The most spectacular of all estuaries—and, at the same time, among the most barren—are fjords. These are deep, narrow, U-shaped gorges carved in mountain valleys by tongues of glacial ice during the ice ages. They occur in high-latitude coastal regions, such as those of Norway and Tierra del Fuego in South America, on the coast of Alaska and along most of the Arctic Canadian coastline. Because of the great weight and thickness of the ice, the glaciers cut into bedrock far below sea level; a fjord may extend inland for scores of miles and is commonly hundreds of yards deep. At the mouth of the mountain valley, the melting glacier typically deposited boulders and clay as it began to retreat, forming a kind of threshold, or sill, on the valley floor. As a result, fjords frequently have shallow entrances that restrict the movement of bottom waters, preventing exchange of the salt water on the seaward side with the fresh water on the landward side, so that only the upper layers of water in a fjord are actually estuarine. Without the renewal of oxygen provided by incoming ocean water, the deep layers of many fjords become oxygen-deficient and consequently devoid of life. This is why Scandinavians cannot make a living fishing in the fjords but must venture far out to offshore banks to find adequate catches.

An estuary is a battleground where the salt sea and the fresh-water river fight for supremacy, with final victory denied to both. As on a real field of battle, the creatures that happen to be in the zone of conflict are imperiled; very few marine creatures can tolerate wide variations in the salinity, temperature or sediment content of their environment, and almost no fresh-water species can survive in salt water. Thus a kind of paradox: The remarkable fecundity of an estuary is, in fact, fragile in the extreme, because it is based on the abundant proliferation of the very few plant, animal and fish species that have been able to adapt to the most dynamic aquatic environment on earth.

The principal determinant of the success and distribution of life in the estuary is salinity. Ocean water contains, on the average, 35 parts per thousand of salts—not only common salt, but 53 others as well. Most of the salts originate in the central rifts of the Mid-Ocean Ridge, the 40,000-mile-long undersea mountain range where new ocean floor is constantly being formed from the molten basalt that wells up from within the earth's mantle and spreads slowly outward from the ridges. As the new crust solidifies, it releases water that was previously imprisoned as vapor in the molten rock and is suffused with many of the 73 elements found in sea water. In all the world's oceans, the variation in dissolved-salt concentration is no greater than two parts per thousand from the average, which itself has not changed for at least 200 million years.

By contrast, the salinity of an estuary ranges across the widest possible spectrum—from fresh water in its upper reaches to sea water at its lower end. The concentrations change from hour to hour, from place to place and from depth to depth, but in general the aquatic denizens of an estuary array themselves according to their abilities to tolerate salinity changes, in distinct patterns that extend from river mouth seaward.

A group of biologists at the Marine Laboratory of Florida State University studied the Apalachicola Bay area on the Gulf of Mexico and correlated the animals found in the estuary with the salinity of their habitats. Snails, mussels and channel catfish, for example, were found only near the head of the estuary, where salinity was less than five parts per thousand. Oysters began to appear a bit farther out, where the salinity was five to 10 parts per thousand, but they were absent beyond the area where salinity was

Rain clouds hover over New Zealand's Milford Sound, a 12-mile-long fjord opening into the Tasman Sea. An annual rainfall of 300 inches floods this unusual estuary with so much runoff that several inches of fresh water may float on top of the denser sea water.

more than 30 parts per thousand. No mature shrimp were found until salinity approached 15 parts per thousand, at about the middle of the estuary. Starfish inhabited the same area. But sturgeon, mullet and blue crabs appeared to roam the estuary at will, thriving in every salinity concentration present.

The same patterning occurs in European estuaries. There, a scud called Gammarus is a prominent member of bottom-fauna communities. Two species of Gammarus are true marine varieties and do not penetrate very far from ocean water. In the shifting salinity of the estuaries, a third species appears, which itself is divided into three subspecies solely on the basis of salinity tolerance. One of the subspecies is found near the seaward end of the estuary, another in the middle, and the third, which can apparently tolerate fresh water some of the time, at the landward end.

Having adapted to a certain range of salinity conditions, such creatures have a difficult time when the tide rushes in and drastically alters the salt concentration with its influx of sea water, or when storms cause the rivers to swell and flood the estuary with fresh water. The salt content of the water at a single spot might vary from that of full sea water to fresh water during a simple flow and ebb of the tide.

Estuarine animals have evolved a truly remarkable array of devices and methods for coping with sudden and extreme changes in salinity. Even one-celled protozoa have devised a fairly complicated means of coping with water that suddenly becomes less salty than they require: In effect, they bail out the unwelcome fresh water, through a small pore, as fast as it comes in. The shells of such crustaceans as shrimp, crabs and lobsters keep out both water and salt. Some bivalves, especially oysters, simply close their shells for a time when the salinity of the water is not to their liking. A salt-water mollusk called the shipworm (because it bores into wood structures under the water line) has an especially ingenious method for protecting itself from fresh water. As the bivalve bores into the timber, it leaves one end of its body sticking out of the opening it has bored. At the end of this tail is a structure called a pallet. If the wood is suddenly flooded with fresh water, the shipworm quickly pulls its pallet into the hole and plugs the hole, keeping it sealed until conditions improve.

Although the salt content of estuarine water generally increases in a seaward direction along its length, there is a great deal more than that to the mingling of sea water and fresh water, and the dynamics of the process are of critical importance to the life that teems beneath the surface. Because fresh water is lighter than salt water, river water entering an estuary overrides the salt water and spreads outward toward the sea. When the flow of the river is substantially stronger than the force of the tides (as, for instance, in the Mississippi delta estuary), the heavier salt water tends to assume the shape of a wedge lying on the estuary floor with its narrow edge toward the river mouth. In this circumstance, relatively little mixing of salt water and fresh water occurs; the water tends to be quite fresh on one side of the demarcation line—the top surface of the wedge—and very salty on the other.

When stronger tides or some other factor increases the friction along the wedge boundary, the salt water begins to ripple just as surface water does in a wind; submarine waves form along the top of the wedge and break down the dividing line by transporting quantities of salt water into the

Four Mixing Modes for Estuaries

All estuaries are arenas for the mixing of fresh and salt water, but the way in which this is accomplished can vary considerably, depending on the relative strengths of the rivers and tides that supply the dual ingredients. Four basic situations occur (right).

Because salt water is denser than fresh, sea water tends to enter an estuary along the bottom while fresh water spreads seaward at or near the surface. As a result, in most estuaries salinity increases with depth and also with distance from the river mouth. The demarcation between the salt and fresh water is most clearly defined when the river flow is much stronger than the tidal currents—as, for instance, at the mouth of the powerful Mississippi River, where Gulf of Mexico tides are relatively modest. In this sort of estuary—known to oceanographers as the highly stratified type—the salt water forms a clearly defined wedge lying on the bottom; the sea water mixes with the fresh water primarily on the wedge's surface.

The stronger tides of the other three types of estuary cause more thorough mixing and corresponding changes in the salinity gradient, or pattern of increasing or decreasing saltiness; when the tides are dominant, there is no vertical gradient and the water is equally salty at the top and the bottom of the estuary at a given point.

The patterns of salinity are also affected, especially in very wide estuaries, by the tendency of the earth's rotation to deflect movement. This Coriolis force causes the fresh water in a Northern Hemisphere estuary to advance seaward along the right-hand shore rather than the left-hand shore, as observed from inland (water in the Southern Hemisphere is deflected to the left).

STRONG RIVER, WEAK TIDE
In a highly stratified estuary, a wedge of sea water *(green)* moves upstream on the bottom of the estuary under the fresh-water flow *(blue)* of a large river. Submarine waves form along the surface of the salt-water wedge; mixing occurs as they break.

A BALANCE OF FORCES
When the volume of the tide approximates or slightly exceeds that of the river flow, turbulence obliterates the outlines of the salt-water wedge. The result is called a partially mixed estuary, in which salinity increases with depth wherever it is measured.

A DOMINANT TIDE
A vertically homogeneous estuary is what results when powerful tides mix the waters so thoroughly that the salinity is equalized from top to bottom. But the Coriolis force tends to deflect fresh water along one shore, creating a lateral salinity gradient.

AN OVERWHELMED RIVER
When the tide overpowers the river, salinity becomes equal from one side of the estuary to the other as well as from top to bottom. In this type of estuary—called sectionally homogeneous—the salinity increases only with distance from the river mouth.

fresh water and vice versa. Such increased mingling has a significance beyond the changed gradient of salinity. The oxygen in the surface fresh water of an estuary tends to be rapidly depleted by the teeming communities of plankton and algae found there, and unless the oxygen is replenished from the supplies available in the sea water, the food chain could be disastrously impoverished.

Two additional types of estuarine mixing are found in estuaries where the strength of the tides, compared with the flow of the incoming river, is greater (*pages 102-103*). When the tides are strong enough to obliterate the salt wedge, the waters mingle along vertical boundaries, the fresh water pushing through and mixing with advancing salt water in columns. The resulting salinity is the same from the surface to the bottom of the water at any one place, and it increases toward the ocean. If the tides are so powerful that they completely overwhelm the river flow, the estuary becomes thoroughly mixed: The vertical columns disappear and salinity evens out not only from top to bottom but from one side to the other, although it still increases to seaward.

These circulation models are neat only in theory; they can be found operating simultaneously in different parts of an estuary and replacing each other from one hour or day to the next in a single section. But even though they are highly simplified, the models, especially the salt-wedge pattern, are useful in understanding both the astounding fertility and the relative impermanence of estuaries. The basic pattern of water movement they describe—seaward near the surface, landward along the bottom—sets up a cycle that tends to entrap both the nutrients that foster plant growth and the riverborne sediments that will eventually obliterate the estuary.

River currents deliver to the estuary a constant supply of such nutrients as phosphorus and nitrogen, most of which are carried by tiny bits of silt. The particles, transported seaward with the surface fresh water, begin to settle as the energy of the river is dissipated. When they sink into the tidal currents near the bottom, the sediments are thrust shoreward once again, shepherded into a high concentration that has dual implications: It creates a rich feast for the creatures at the base of the estuary's food chain, and it hastens the inevitable replacement of the estuary with a silted-in delta or salt marsh.

Human activities have added to the sediment load being carried by many of the world's rivers, with unfortunate consequences for estuaries. Deforestation increased the siltation of the estuary at the mouth of the Betsiboka River in Madagascar so greatly that an entire harbor dredged during World War II has completely filled in. Every time a lot is cleared and a basement excavated so a home can be built near the Chesapeake Bay, some four tons of additional sediment end up in the water. As Jerome Williams, a professor of oceanography at the U.S. Naval Academy, put it, "Fewer trees, more construction, more parking lots, more runoff—just about everything man does stirs up the water. If you want a pristine bay, then forget about people."

Whatever else an estuary may be, it is never pristine. Unlike a clear mountain stream or the crystalline waters of the Caribbean, an estuary is a soupy caldron of life. Near the surface, microscopic, free-floating plants called phytoplankton grow and bloom in the light and warmth of the sun, providing a meal for the tiny animals, or zooplankton, that float with them. Aquatic plants, such as the marsh grasses that fringe the estuary, make an important contribution to the food chain, but the fundamental source of fecundity in these waters is the phytoplankton. Only plants, capturing the energy of sunlight in the process known as photosynthesis, can transform inorganic nutrients into organic tissue.

The astronomical numbers of plankton present in an estuary constitute an enormous floating food factory, but the factory can function only where the sun's rays reach. In a silt-laden estuary such as the Chesapeake Bay, this depth is limited on the average to about one tenth the reach of sunlight into the open ocean, yet the output of the Chesapeake's food factory is up to 100 times that of the ocean because the supply of nutrients is so much greater.

The consumers of the bounty range from the minute plankton through various crustaceans, fish and shellfish to the more exotic sting rays and octopods that cruise the gloom of the deep estuary. Noteworthy among the tinier inhabitants of the Chesapeake are the copepods—crustaceans that, when magnified, resemble something between a cockroach and a hairy shrimp. Their population density is such that a bathtub full of Bay water would contain an estimated three million copepods. They are filter feeders, sucking as much as a quart of water every day and straining from it the nutrients they need. Biologists who study these energetic crustaceans note that, if the water they process could somehow be removed from the Bay as the creatures expel it and not be replaced, the Chesapeake would be empty within a few days.

On all sides, regeneration abounds. There are estuarine species of sponges that come equipped with a sort of immortality capsule called a gemmule. When an adult sponge dies and begins to decay, the gemmule, encased in a resilient membrane, is released from the rotting corpse and settles on the estuary floor. Eventually the case ruptures, and new sponge cells are freed to join others in assembling a new sponge. Another gemmule strain, found in saltier water, is equipped with a coating of oscillating hairs. Instead of waiting for the parent to rot, these infant cells are free to leave at an earlier stage, and they row about the estuary with their hairs until they find a suitable anchorage.

In the unique environs of estuarine waters are found many intriguing departures from biological norms. One example is the pipefish, which is related to and resembles a sea horse. In the creature's reproductive cycle, the female pipefish places her eggs in a pouch on the male's abdomen by means of a long tube that she extrudes from her body. Inside the pouch, the eggs are fertilized by sperm, and the hatching of several hundred pipefish babies becomes the responsibility of the male parent. The mother simply swims away. When gestation is completed, the pouch splits open and the new generation pours forth, leaving the father pipefish free to get his figure back.

Even the most familiar of the residents of the crowded estuary turn out, on close examination, to lead secret lives of astonishing complexity. A case in point is the common oyster. Four or five times each summer, adult female oysters release up to 100,000 eggs each into the waters of the Chesapeake Bay, and male oysters eject billions of sperm. Only a few of the eggs will encounter sperm and become fertilized, and only

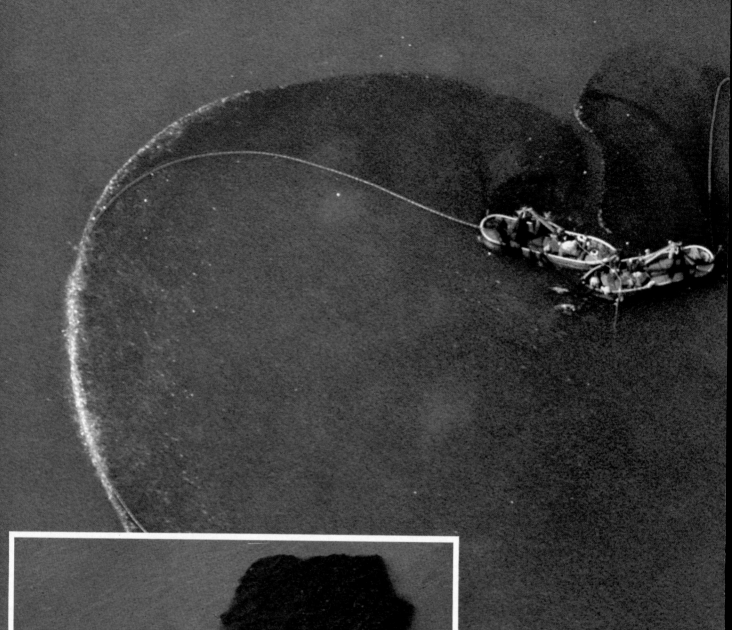

Spotted from the air for pursuing fishermen, a
school of menhaden (*left*) migrates from a South
Carolina estuary toward summer feeding
grounds off New England. The fish are caught
with a 1,200-foot-long net, paid out from
two boats that encircle the menhaden (*above*).

about one in 10,000 of the fertilized eggs will survive the larval stage.

For about two weeks after the fertilized eggs have developed into larvae, the young oysters float in the restless currents of the Bay. Their growing shells drag them ever closer to the bottom, and by the end of the two weeks, their life's travels are almost over. In the process of settling down, however, the young oysters exert a surprising degree of control over their destiny.

When the larval oyster first settles to the bottom, it promptly extends its specially adapted foot and gropes about in the muck for a solid foundation; if the oyster is to survive as it grows, it must avoid sinking into the soft sediments, where it would smother. If it cannot find a rock, an old oyster shell or some other satisfactory support, the larva uses a group of hairlike appendages called cilia to flog itself back up into the water to drift to a new location. After it finds a suitably hard place, it secretes a drop of glue from its remarkable foot, applies the glue to the chosen foundation, turns, presses its left shell into the glue and holds its position for 15 minutes, until the glue sets. The oyster is then anchored for the rest of its life.

The oyster may be immobile, but it is far from inactive. Its first order of business is to absorb its own foot, for which it has no further use. From then on, it subsists by forcing water through its gills, at a rate of up to 10 gallons per hour, and filtering out every morsel of nutrition therein. If the salinity of the water falls too low, or the sediment concentration gets too high, or the water becomes too cold or too warm, the oyster seals itself tightly and waits for better conditions. Otherwise, its existence consists of pumping and filtering—and an intriguing sex life.

During cold weather the oyster's body is composed mostly of fatty tissue and salts in a combination that is highly pleasing to most human palates (although Jonathan Swift marveled at the boldness of the first man to eat one of these bivalves). But the warmth of spring brings with it a powerful urge to procreate, which the oyster heeds with unrivaled thoroughness. It first chooses a sex to assume for the coming season—its options include male, female or a little of both—and converts 80 per cent of its body weight to the appropriate sex organ. When this transformation has been accomplished, the body tissue is thin, watery and tasteless; hence oysters are harvested only during the cold months of the year, before the reproductive process gets under way.

The high infant mortality rate suffered by oysters is typical of estuarine shellfish: To maintain their populations in this difficult environment, prodigality in reproduction is essential. Estuarine fish have adopted the same strategy, with a consequent productivity that is a wonder to any who contemplate its dimensions.

A simple statistical comparison can serve to define the phenomenon: Georges Bank, off Cape Cod, one of the world's best fishing grounds, yields less than three tons of fish per square mile per year; the annual harvest from a square mile of the Chesapeake Bay is almost 12 tons. Certain varieties of fish not only spend part of their lives in estuaries but often, after having traveled great distances, return to them. Salmon, for instance, may travel from North American rivers to the waters of Greenland and back during the course of their lives. Biologists keep accounts of the energy expenditures and energy resources inherent in animal adaptations, and they expect the books to balance. Although definitive studies have not been done, it

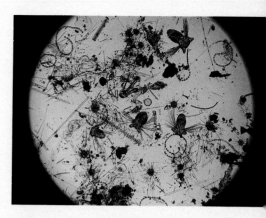

A drop of water from North Carolina's Bogue Sound, enlarged 10 times, teems with the tiny plants (phytoplankton) and animals (zooplankton) that nourish the estuary's small crustaceans and fingerling fish. Here, three whiskery nauplius zooplankton *(center)* graze on chlorophyll-tinted phytoplankton.

appears that, despite the energy required to adapt to the changeable estuarine environment and to travel great distances to reach it, the fish are more than compensated by the energy that is available from the estuary's bounteous nutrients.

The adjustments that estuarine species make to their ecological twilight zone are endlessly ingenious. Such fish as the salmon, which lives in salt water but spawns in fresh, has developed biological defenses against extreme changes in salinity: highly active kidneys, special salt glands in the gills, and an almost impermeable skin. The low freezing point of saline water presents another challenge. During the cold months of the year, especially in shallow bays, saline water has the capacity to freeze a fish's blood; however, the winter flounder has developed the ability to alter its blood-serum chemistry, thus lowering the temperature at which its blood will freeze.

All of this evolutionary legerdemain fades in comparison with another adaptive technique of the flounder, which at birth looks and swims like any other fish. But soon, to prepare for its life of feeding in the shallows, the flounder begins to swim on its side; and to maximize its vision in this position, one of its eyes migrates across its head to join the other eye on what has become the fish's top side.

Among the fish found in the Chesapeake, the striped bass, or rockfish, has made perhaps the most complete and successful transition from the open sea to the estuarine environment. Other varieties—shad, alewife and herring—use the fresher waters at the head of the Bay for spawning, and then

Eelgrass combed out by the retreating tide lies at the edge of a California estuary. Animals as diverse as snails and geese feed on the plant, whose long, narrow leaves also provide shelter for many other species.

return to the ocean; but 90 per cent of the bass remain in the Bay for their entire lives. With adult females reaching six feet in length and weighing 175 pounds, the striped bass has become the leading commercial fish of the Chesapeake.

The abundance of marine life in estuaries such as the Chesapeake makes it easy to forget that the creatures thriving there are highly vulnerable to sudden change. This fragility was highlighted in 1972, when Hurricane Agnes came ashore over the Eastern seaboard and dumped heavy rains on the area that is drained by Chesapeake tributaries. For 10 days during and after the storm, the Susquehanna flowed into the Bay at a rate that was 15 times greater than normal, drastically lowering the salinity of the estuary. An estimated two million bushels of oysters, which can tolerate low salinity for only a brief period, were killed, along with almost all of the Bay's clams.

Less dramatic, but of far greater import for the future of the Chesapeake, are the worrisome, long-term changes affecting a basic element of the food chain—the grasses. Many forms of life are dependent upon these grasses for their survival—fish, plants, mollusks and crustaceans. But humans are disrupting the equation. Wherever agricultural land is drained by rivers, the rivers carry away traces of fertilizer, mainly nitrogen and phosphorus, along with the runoff. The fertilizers stimulate blooming algae—free-floating mats of growth that use the oxygen in the water and cut off sunlight to submerged grasses. Moreover, when the algae die and decompose, the bacteria they generate consume even more of the oxygen needed by plants and fish.

On September 30, 1982, the Environmental Protection Agency published a comprehensive report on the ecology in the Chesapeake, the result of six years of research. The report pointed to a limitation of sunlight,

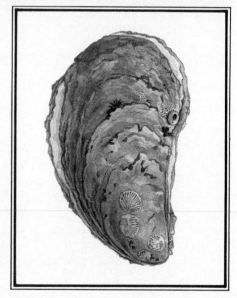

Chesapeake Bay watermen pluck oysters from the bottom with long-handled tongs while a co-worker sorts the day's catch (*upper picture*). Each rough-edged, curving ridge on an oyster's shell (*above*) represents one season's growth.

caused by nutrient enrichment, as the primary culprit in giving the water a murky quality and depriving the vital submerged grasses of the oxygen they require. Thus, curiously, the problem is not so much that the Bay is dying, but that where the vast proliferation of algae is concerned, it is too much alive.

Sometime during the past three decades, submerged grasses have vanished from the upper and middle parts of the Bay. Evidence suggests that some kind of wholesale extinction occurred in the late 1960s in what one plant geographer has described as "a unique event within the last 1,000 years." Although the connection is not certain, concentrations of nitrogen and phosphorus have roughly doubled in the upper half of the Bay during the same time frame.

The decline of the grasses has had a detrimental effect on oysters, clams and fish that feed on the fine debris of decomposing grasses; on the striped bass that feed on organisms flourishing in the grasses; and on the birds that feed both on the grasses themselves and on animals foraging among them. In fact, according to one study, there is a connection between the disappearance of the grasses and a great decline in migrating canvasback, redhead, and goldeneye ducks.

Meanwhile, though, bluefish, menhaden and other species that thrive on the algae blooms have been steadily increasing. This has led some observers to conclude that the ecology of the Bay is merely evolving. "The Bay will always be in balance," says one oceanographer. "It will always have water and life. The water may be polluted and the only fish may be carp, but it will always be in balance."

Whatever the threat of the long-term trends at work in the Chesapeake, there is reassurance in the ancient turning of the seasons and the regular response of the creatures of the estuary. And none of them has a busier calendar of annual events than the blue crab. Shortly after emerging in the

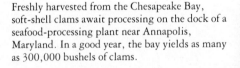

Freshly harvested from the Chesapeake Bay, soft-shell clams await processing on the dock of a seafood-processing plant near Annapolis, Maryland. In a good year, the bay yields as many as 300,000 bushels of clams.

The blue crab's three pairs of walking legs equip it for travel on sandy or muddy estuary bottoms; and its flexible swimming legs, which end in flattened, paddle-shaped joints, permit it to swim sideways or backward with ease. Often a scavenger, the crab uses its heavily muscled claws to tear at dead organic matter.

springtime from the Bay's depths, a female crab may eject two million fertilized eggs from her body. She attaches them to the shell on her abdomen and carries the spongy mass for a month, feeding herself ravenously in order to be able to nurture them. Then, sometime in June, she flexes her abdominal apron and releases the dark mass into the water. Throughout the spawning grounds, which are located in the southern reaches of the Bay near the capes, billions of minute larvae swarm upward through the sun-warmed water to take up the struggle for existence among the plankton and the predators that teem in their watery universe. The larvae are easy prey; of each two million eggs fertilized, an average of only two will survive to adulthood.

Summer is mating time for crabs, and for them the process is rather more complicated than for most animals. Impregnation of the female is possible only for a short time after she has shed her shell, as all crabs must do periodically to accommodate their growth. Watermen can tell when a crab is about to molt—and become the prized delicacy known as a soft-shell crab: The feathery edge of one segment of the crab's swimming leg turns red. Whether by this sign or not, the male crab knows when a potential mate is about to shed, and he carefully but firmly grasps the female's shell and carries her until shedding occurs. So intent is the male on his purpose that he will not release his grip even if he is caught and hoisted aboard a boat.

The pair finds a secluded spot, and in due time the female is impregnated. Afterward, the male stays with her, cradling her as before until her new shell has hardened and she is able to go her way. By August, the mating activity reaches a peak and the females are in the midst of their own migration—down the Bay to the spawning area, where they will spend the winter months. Males do not return to the spawning area, and thus for much of the year the crab population of the Bay is largely segregated, with the males tending to gather in the northern shallows and the females in the southern depths.

The sexes also differ in their responses in impending death. Males, it is thought, clamber down into the depths of the ancient submarine river channels of the Bay when they sense the time to die; but aged females form up in yet another seasonal crab migration. At the end of what their instincts tell them has been their last summer, they leave their spawning grounds, often in great numbers, and for the first time in their lives leave the estuary—to die in the primal sea where their distant ancestors once lived. They can guess wrong, of course. Every year a few elderly, barnacle-encrusted females return from their sojourns at sea to haunt their estuarine homes for a little while longer.

In September, the murky water slowly begins to cool, and the flow of the rivers from parched summer fields slackens. With the resistance of the fresh water weakened, the tidal currents probe farther landward along the bottom, bringing much-needed oxygen to replenish water that has provided for the needs of the flourishing plankton and algae all summer long. As the surface waters cool, they become heavier, sinking and mingling with the salt water below, distributing the microscopic life of the Bay more uniformly through its waters.

The circumstances convey another imperative signal to the blue crab. All over the Chesapeake, the crabs begin to slide off the shoals and head for the middle of the Bay, downward into the ancient bed of the Susquehanna, to depths of 100 feet or more. Safe from the reach of the coldest winter, they work themselves backward into the soft silt at an angle of 45 degrees, squirming into the mud until only their eye stalks and antennae remain exposed, and there they sleep until spring. Ω

Chapter 4

THE ROLE OF THE WETLANDS

Visitors to the 289-square-mile island of Camargue—the heart of the Rhone River delta in southern France—tend to be stunned by its initial impact. Against a starkly beautiful backdrop of mud and salt flats, a parade of strange images meets the eye: herds of wild white horses; bands of colorful gypsies; scores of horsemen bearing trident-like prods as they gallop across the flats, herding black bulls that resemble creatures depicted on some ancient Greek vase; spirited bullfights in arenas dating from the Roman occupation. And, as if all this were not exotic enough, the region also harbors the Continent's largest flocks of flamingos.

Basically an estuarine delta, the Camargue is a triangle of built-up silt lying between the two branches of the Rhone—the Grand Rhône and the Petit Rhône—that flow into the bulge of the Mediterranean Sea called the Gulf of Lion. The delta is composed almost totally of alluvium rinsed from the watershed of the river, which springs violently from the glaciers of the Swiss Alps, then slows abruptly as it hits the plains. By the time it reaches the city of Arles, some 40 miles from the coast, the Rhone flows at a stately pace, carrying mostly fine silt from the 20 million tons of material scoured from its banks each year—enough, say the guidebooks, to cover all of Paris in a silt blanket more than 10 inches thick.

As a result of siltation at the river's mouth, the Camargue delta extends from 30 to 45 feet farther into the Mediterranean each year. But, as with most of the sea's edges, the picture here is far from simple: The level of the Mediterranean basin is slowly rising, encroaching upon and eroding the shoreline. Stes.-Maries-de-la-Mer, the unofficial capital of the Camargue and once an inland city, is now buttressed by breakwaters; and Faraman Lighthouse, which stood 757 yards from the water in 1840, was finally engulfed by the sea near the end of World War I and had to be replaced.

The estuarine heart of the Camargue—much of it set aside as a nature preserve—is frequently called Western Europe's last remaining wilderness area, and with good reason. Abutting the featureless beaches that meet the sea to the south is a belt of sand dunes, sparsely tufted with patchy clumps of resilient marram grass and an occasional brightly tinted flower. Behind the dunes lie stretches of bleak salt steppes, their bitter soil hospitable only to the hardiest of plants, among them glassworts and, farther inland, tassel pondweed, which thrives underwater. This is a valuable adaptation in the wild Camargue, where some 65 per cent of the territory is covered by water during even the driest seasons, and torrential winter rains bring the total of submerged land to about 90 per cent. Deeper into the Camargue, closer to

Atlantic tides flow through a narrow inlet and into the maze of creeks incised in a New Jersey salt marsh. Sand dunes shield the wetlands from rough water and help to create a favorable environment for cord grass, which grows along the coast from Maine to Florida.

A herd of wild horses splashes across a flooded marsh toward a shrubby hummock in southern France's low-lying Camargue. Similar herds have inhabited these wetlands for at least 2,000 years.

the Rhone and its great flows of fresh water, the soil's salt content declines until brackish lakes give way to fresh-water ponds and soils that can support a wide variety of terrestrial plant life.

If the wildest sections of the Camargue are unsuitable for human habitation, they are ideal environments for the vast numbers of wild creatures that thrive there, protected from the encroachments of modern civilization. Some 200 species of birds can be seen in the Camargue, among them year-round residents such as yellow buntings, water rails and black-headed warblers, as well as seasonal visitors such as nightingales, crimson herons and whistling ducks. Snakes, lizards and frogs also thrive in the delta, as do such mammals as boars, foxes and hares.

With its sweeping vistas of uninhabited marshlands and brackish, shallow lakes called *étangs,* and with its colorful array of wildlife, the Camargue is one of the most striking examples of the world's coastal wetlands—the strange intermediate zones at the edges of many seashores and estuaries. At the same time aquatic and terrestrial, these wetlands are too frequently submerged—either by the tides or by flooding—to be called land, and too frequently exposed to be called bodies of water.

Tide ranges in the Mediterranean are moderate to almost nonexistent, so the water that saturates and fills the Camargue's salt-laden lowlands comes mainly from seasonal rains. However, in most other parts of the world,

including the shores of northern Europe and North America, the tide range is far greater, and coastal wetlands are washed by the incessant ebb and flow of tidal waters. Having slipped through inlets, past headlands and open beaches, into embayments and up river entrances, into hundreds of winding creeks and sheltered coves, the sea's final surge of tidal power is spent. It slows on sandy flats, eddies farther inland through expanses of mud and at last eases to a stop amid grassy salt marshes or, in the tropics, in dense mangrove swamps. Shallow, mosquito-ridden and inhospitable to human life in their natural state, tidal wetlands have traditionally been seen as perhaps the least desirable of coastal features. Yet their unprepossessing appearance disguises a unique and intricate environment.

These wetlands are saturated not only by the tides but by rivers and streams. As the fresh-water runoff arrives in the wetlands, its flow is retarded. Water seeps into the ground and is held there, thus replenishing the vital groundwater supplies that have been depleted in so many areas by the demands of industry and agriculture. Where they have been allowed to remain as barriers between the sea and coastal communities, salt marshes and mangrove swamps stabilize shorelines by absorbing floodwater and releasing it slowly, thus providing a self-repairing natural protection against surging storm waves.

The creatures of the wetlands constitute one of the earth's richest ag-

glomerations of living organisms. Wading birds, migratory waterfowl and small mammals abound in the shallows and flats at low tide, looking for oysters, crabs and other creatures that inhabit the nearshore waters. Alligators patrol subtropical marshlands and mangrove swamps, waiting for the unwary raccoon or muskrat arriving to dine, say, on fiddler crabs. At low tide, the muddy bottoms of tidal creeks and the broad expanses of tide-flat sediments display the signatures of many resident species, from the random squiggles of marine worms to the meandering tracks of birds. Most of the marks are easily categorized, but others tax the imagination: For example, one might be hard put to conjure the creature that could leave the horseshoe crab's distinctive trail, which suggests the passage of a small bulldozer pulling a plow, with small creatures skittering along either side on tiptoe.

Other, more conspicuous tracks, geometric patterns of waves, ripples and rills, are left on the tide flats by shallow tidal currents. Precisely how the water creates these marks is unclear. Some of the water's imprints in the sand, of a type generally called backwash ripples, are similar in form, proportion and interval to water-wave patterns and run roughly parallel to the line of advance and retreat of the tides over the flats. Other marks, complex diamond patterns called rhomboid marks, occasionally appear precise enough to have been placed by a tile setter. At the top of each diamond is an inverted V shape similar to the swash mark produced by passage of a sheet of water over a pebble lying in sand. However, as Paul Komar, a marine geologist at Oregon State University, has noted: "In the case of most rhomboid marks there are no noticeable objects visible on the beach." These markings remain a sort of tidal message written in a code as yet uncracked.

Tidal wetlands are shaped as well as sustained by the delicate interaction of land and sea. Their lower boundaries are sandy, gravelly or even stony, because the scouring tides wash away finer sediments. Farther up the shore, the terrain becomes muddy; the tide has less and less energy, and it lets even the finest grains fall from its grip to settle out along the bottom.

When enough mud accumulates, vegetation appears. Once the plants gain a foothold, they trap the sediments flowing past them and slow the currents even further, causing still more sediment to settle. The vegetation

Each pile of sand castings on this mud flat marks one opening of a lugworm's U-shaped burrow. The greenish, eight-inch-long worm swallows water and sand, digests whatever organic matter is contained in the mixture, and then excretes the remainder.

thickens and spreads. When the plants die, they decay and form peat deposits. The land beneath an established tidal marsh consists mostly of peat—a mat of plant roots and stem fibers, plus silt and decayed vegetation and material brought in from the sea by the tides and trapped amid the roots. In some areas, marsh peat has been building up for thousands of years, and it is not unusual to find deposits that measure 20 feet or more in thickness. Peat can absorb more than its own weight in water, leaving it springy when the tide is out and gelatinous as the tide rises.

As the salt-marsh vegetation spreads and the peat deposits continue to accumulate, the area of the marsh grows. Eventually, its landward portion is far enough from the sea to avoid all but the highest spring tides. In this zone, known as the high marsh, such fresh-water plants as wild celery, cattails and wild rice take root. Closer to the water, in the low marsh, the tide-washed terrain is populated by plant types that neatly arrange themselves according to the length of exposure to salt water. Only the lowest tides leave the low marsh uncovered, so the plants have just a few hours every two weeks when their roots are above water level. In the extensive salt marshes of the eastern United States, the distinguishing growth is a spiky cord grass called *Spartina alterniflora,* uncontested king of the marsh grasses, which can reach nine feet in height. A similar cord grass, *Spartina towsendii,* occurs in European salt marshes.

Spartina alterniflora is a halophyte—a land plant singularly able to survive with its roots soaked in salt water. It flourishes in the nominally inhospitable tide-marsh environment by means of an extraordinary membrane that filters most of the salt from the tidal waters entering its root system. What is more, any salt that manages to seep through this membrane is excreted by a glandular backup system located on the leaves: White flecks of salt are a distinctive mark of cord-grass leaves at low tide.

Nor is that the end of *Spartina alterniflora's* resiliency. The pores through which the leaves ooze excess salt also serve a respiratory function, breathing in supplemental oxygen and passing it directly back to the roots through a minute piping system. This oxygen renewal compensates for depletion of oxygen along the marsh floor by bacteria in the process of breaking down dead plant matter. When tidewater rises over the leaves, the oxygen-intake system shuts down; the leaf pores close, and the plant is literally saved from drowning in salt water that otherwise would be drawn in through its auxiliary breathing apparatus.

In tropical climates, some salt-marsh grasses are replaced by mangrove trees. Mangroves have extensive root systems that form dense thickets at or beneath the water level and provide shelter for both marine and land ani-

THE TYPES OF TIDAL WETLANDS
Tides delineate the three major subdivisions of coastal wetlands. The tide flats, which abut the constantly submerged sea floor, are inundated almost all the time and are exposed only by extreme low tides; the low marsh is flooded by every high tide; the high marsh is covered only by extreme high tides.

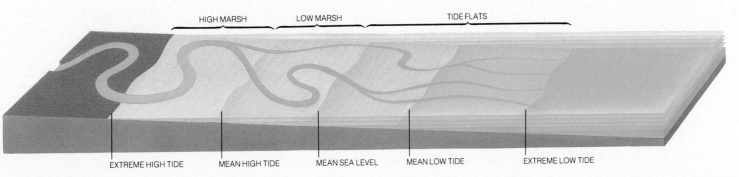

HIGH MARSH   LOW MARSH   TIDE FLATS

EXTREME HIGH TIDE   MEAN HIGH TIDE   MEAN SEA LEVEL   MEAN LOW TIDE   EXTREME LOW TIDE

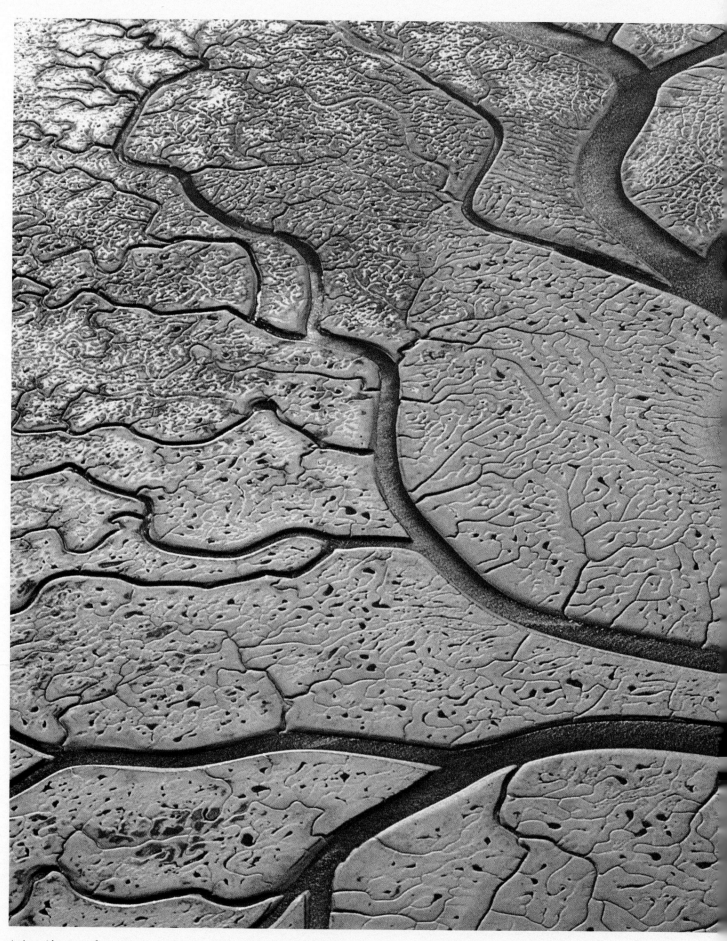

At low tide, water flows across a California mud flat toward the Pacific Ocean through the numerous branching channels of a dendritic drainage system.

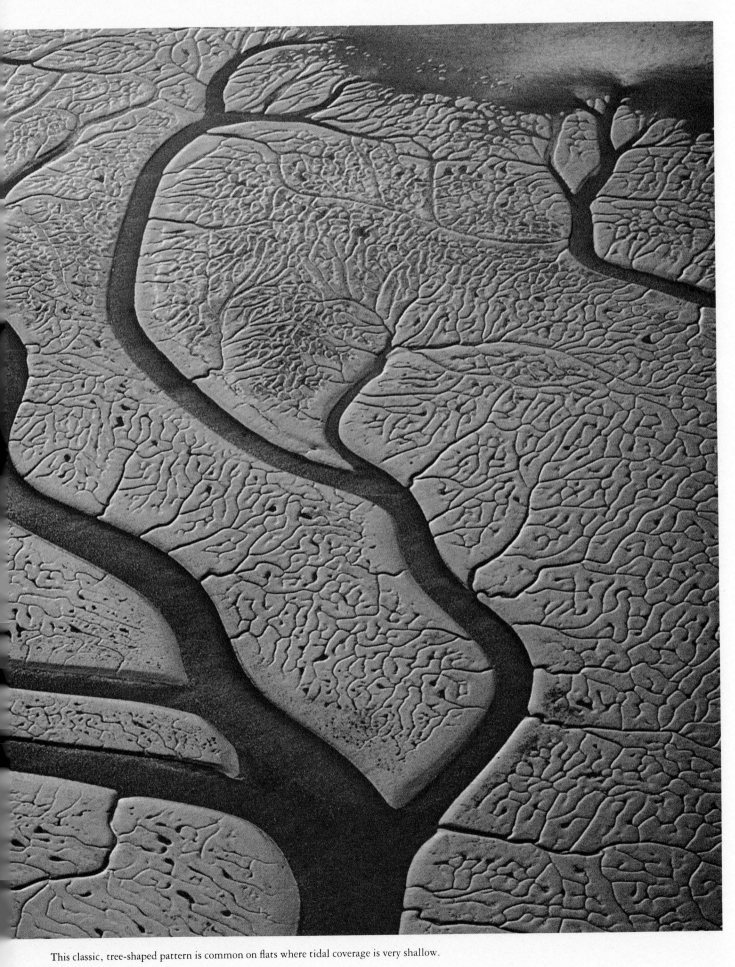

This classic, tree-shaped pattern is common on flats where tidal coverage is very shallow.

121

mals, some of which are particularly adapted to the mangrove environments. One such species is the mangrove oyster, which attaches itself to roots and branches exposed at low tide, thus presenting the unusual spectacle of oysters seeming to grow on trees. Because they can trap sediments so effectively, mangroves often serve to build up valuable land. In the vast coastal swamps of the Biscayne Bay and Florida Bay regions, for example, mangroves have been responsible for adding 1,500 acres of new land to the Florida coastline over the past 40 years.

The mangrove may do its part as a land builder, but the Spartina grass is the key to the incredible productivity of a marsh. Where *Spartina alterniflora* flourishes, all marsh creatures are almost totally dependent on it. Only a small amount, perhaps 10 per cent, of the standing grass is eaten—mainly by salt-marsh grasshoppers and a few snail species. The rest is reworked by bacteria into decay products, or detritus, which feed a legion of marine species that are consumed in turn by other, still larger, animals.

As cord grass dries, it becomes brittle, breaking off just above the root line and dropping into the tidewater. There, fungi and bacteria fall quickly to work and reduce the fragments into a sort of organic soup that feeds huge colonies of zooplankton and, in its various mixtures with bacteria and algae, also nourishes a wide assortment of flies, crabs and snails; an array of filter feeders such as clams, mussels, oysters and crustaceans; flatfish such as sole and flounder; striped bass, or rockfish; and so-called industrial fish such as mullet and menhaden. Ranked number one among commercial fish taken along the Atlantic coast of the United States, menhaden are not consumed directly as food but are used in the manufacture of protein animal feeds and fertilizers, as well as in the production of ingredients essential to the making of soap, ink, paint and lubricants.

The most fertile stands of *Spartina alterniflora* have been calculated to yield as much as 10 tons of dry material per acre each year, greater than the yield of an average rice field and equal to that of the best hayfields. And this level of productivity is maintained entirely without human assistance. Tides fertilize the crop by bringing in nutrients dissolved in water; in effect, they also weed, since their salt content excludes all but the halophytes from the low marshes. Much of the rich Spartina-detritus mixture is ingested by animals living in the heart of the marsh, but some flows with the ebbing tide out into the deeper reaches of estuaries or lagoons. And many scientists are convinced that the mixture is moved well beyond these waters and into the open ocean, there to feed a broad variety of marine creatures.

As common as it is in the East, *Spartina alterniflora* is not seen on the Pacific coast of North America. A relative, *Spartina folioso,* or California cord grass, grows in San Francisco Bay and as far south as Baja California, but it lacks the regenerative properties of *Spartina alterniflora* and is therefore not nearly so widespread.

Farther up the coast, the rocky shores, greater tide ranges and pounding surf of the Pacific Northwest generally provide no opportunity for the formation of fertile salt marshes. But there is no shortage of lush vegetation in many of the region's estuaries, where tide flats extend far into the tidal zone. Here, much of the plant life is of a kind that marine biologists call nonemergent, another way of saying that it grows essentially underwater. During spring and summer, many of the Northwestern tide flats are virtually clogged with sea lettuce, kelp and other submarine plants that are all

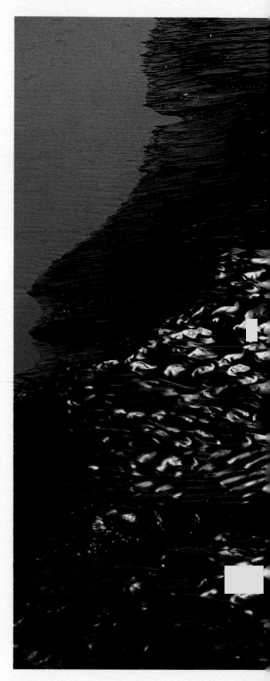

At low tide, a silt flat bordering an Alaskan fjord is evidence of the continual working of the waves and tidal currents with a maze of two-inch-high ripples, some arranged in neat ranks and some *(center left)* shaped like horseshoes.

but invisible to the casual onshore observer. The material withers and disappears in the fall, but not before producing as much as five tons of organic matter per acre. "It may not be what we are used to thinking of as vegetation," says Jefferson J. Gonor, an associate professor of oceanography at Oregon State University, "but it's one of the richest per-unit systems of any in the world."

For all their productivity, coastal wetlands have long been among the world's most abused and exploited natural features. Until relatively recently, in fact, most people considered tide flats and salt marshes to be eyesores that stood in the way of coastal development. The marshes, especially, were seen as evil-smelling, mosquito-ridden places, crawling with slimy organ-

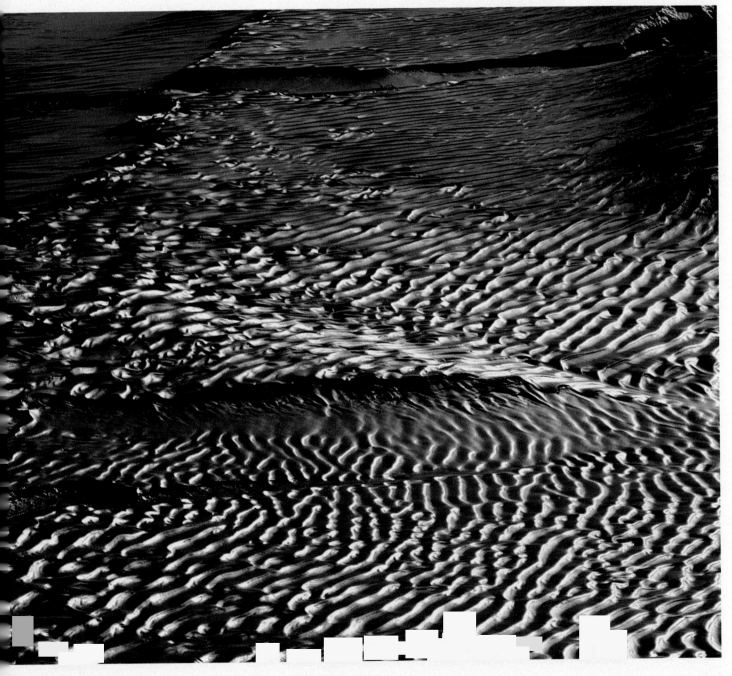

isms, boding nothing at all good for humankind. They were treacherous for children and worthless for grazing animals. Filling in a tidal marsh, in fact, was—and in many places still is—looked upon as environmental improvement. Over the years, many marshes have been converted to garbage dumps, industrial parks, marinas, airports, shopping centers, parks, playgrounds and condominium developments.

The Camargue region of France, while it still retains much of its wild beauty, has hardly been spared from the steady encroachment of civilization. Its bleak flats have been used for agriculture since the Middle Ages, when farmers built rudimentary dikes to hold back the waters of the Rhone. These barriers were no match for severe storms and flooding, but most of the farmsteads, or *mas,* existing today in the Camargue were established between the 16th and 18th Centuries as small enclaves, intermittently overwhelmed by flood. Permanent and effective diking along the Rhone was put in place during the 1850s, and this was followed by a network of irrigation and drainage canals and ditches that made possible the flushing of the salt-laden flatlands by the Rhone currents from the north.

Agriculture has become a big business in the Camargue, and the expansive rice fields in the northern sectors of the delta, developed during the market shortages that followed World War II, now produce enough rice to supply the entire French market. Although such large-scale farming has certainly modified and domesticated the look of the land along the banks of the two Rhones, it has not done lasting harm to wildlife there. Some environmentalists have expressed concern about the rice growers' uses of toxic chemicals that drain into marshes inhabited by large numbers of birds, but other than that, the rice fields are not a detriment to wildfowl; in fact, egrets and ducks spend considerable time in them. In recent years, even flamingos have made unprecedented appearances in the rice fields. In May 1978, for example, growers noted that several dozen of the big pink creatures were setting down to wade in fields recently flooded with fresh water and seeded. Soon there were hundreds of the birds, then thousands, all arriving at dusk and leaving the next morning to return to the salt marshes.

Previously, all species of flamingos had been known to avoid fresh water and to feed almost exclusively on plankton and bottom-feeding organisms found only in brackish shallows. After considerable research, scientists in the Camargue decided that the aberrant behavior—which came during a boom period in the delta's flamingo population, partially the result of two years of drought in the saline lakes of North Africa—occurred because fresh-water runoff from heavy spring rains had filled the salt ponds to unprecedented depths. Finding the water in many places too deep to permit their accustomed manner of feeding, the flamingos readily turned to the unfamiliar fresh-water rice fields.

Rice fields are not the only new element civilization has introduced to the Camargue wetlands over the years. Along with such other additions as roadways and electric power lines, there is also a thriving salt industry on the southeastern edge of the delta. This enterprise is centered around a string of so-called salt pans, shallow lagoons through which sea water is successively pumped and evaporated until, in the harvesting areas, it crystallizes into a crust perhaps four inches thick. Then, usually in September, modern machinery takes over from nature to scoop up the salt and pile it into huge mounds for shipment to refining plants. But even the salt pans, part of the

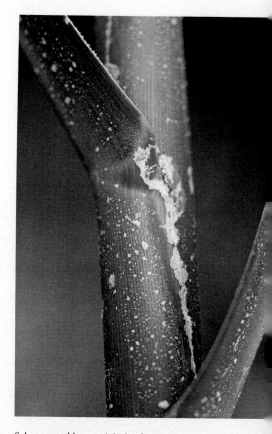

Salt excreted by special glands crusts the leaves and stems of smooth cord grass, *Spartina alterniflora.* Because it can purge itself of the salt absorbed through its roots, cord grass can thrive in a marine environment that is hostile to most plant species.

Wind blowing across a Cape Cod marsh sculpts fine-leaved cord grass, *Spartina patens*, into swirls and hillocks. Also known as salt hay, and once widely cultivated for cattle fodder, this species grows in areas that are flooded only at high tide.

largest saltworks system in Europe, are cherished feeding grounds of several species of wading birds, notably avocets, gulls and flamingos.

Many of the birds that frequent the rice fields and salt pans of the Camargue are drawn by the 40-square-mile Zoological and Botanical Reserve that nestles at the heart of the delta wetlands. Established in the 1920s, this carefully protected wildlife refuge is a spring and summer stopover point for migrating flocks of purple herons, ospreys, plovers, swallows and avocets, and a winter feeding ground for a wide variety of the waterfowl of northern Europe. It is also the summer habitat of tens of thousands of pink flamingos, known locally as firebirds.

But the reserve is more than a mere bird sanctuary. It is a symbol of the determination of the residents of the Camargue to defend and preserve the area's primitive character. Ambitious plans have been afoot since the late 18th Century to dam and dike the entire delta, purge its rich silts of salt and put the whole region under cultivation. Such schemes have invariably been frustrated by the stubborn Camarguais. But the past three decades have seen the natives yielding to the push and pace of an expanding population and the tourism engendered by the region's splendid 30-mile stretch of Mediterranean beach front.

Commenting on some of the recent transformations, the writer and photographer Karl Weber, an authority on the Camargue, noted the initial disappointment of many a new arrival in the region. "He came to see vast unspoilt steppes—and he finds surfaced roads, giant high-voltage pylons and barbed-wire fences stretching for mile after mile. He seeks, perhaps without realizing it, that Camargue which the lonely wanderer a quarter of a century ago might still have found." Weber went on to maintain, however, that the old Camargue is still there. In effect, it exists in seclusion. To

Colonies of mangroves spread like tentacles into the salt-rimmed mud flats of the tropical Morehead River estuary in northeast Australia. The mangroves' arching prop roots *(inset)* lend the trees stability in the soft, tide-shifted mud and, by trapping sediment, help build the ground above the reach of the tides.

ensure their survival, the wild wetlands have been placed beyond the reach of casual tourists. Many of the rare and timid bird species breed precisely during the peak tourist season, and access to the Zoological and Botanical Reserve is generally restricted to accredited persons able to prove a legitimate scientific reason for their visit. An adjacent nature reserve, Les Impériaux, is similarly restricted.

Yet there are viewing points at the edge of the reserves, and a telescope for public use stands on the Digue de la Mer, the dike overlooking the flamingo nesting grounds at the Étang du Frangassier. Many birds have become indifferent to the presence of visitors and can be observed at close range as they feed in the brackish shallows.

The Camargue and its marshes and salt flats are not the only European wetlands threatened by civilization's advance. Others are the Danube delta on the Rumanian shore of the Black Sea; Las Marismas, the tidal marshlands where Spain's Guadalquivir River disgorges into the Gulf of Cádiz; and the delta formed where the Volga River meets the Caspian Sea in the U.S.S.R.

The immense Danube delta—2,000 square miles, including the earth's largest expanse of reed beds—is perhaps the least menaced at the moment, even though the river has for generations been acknowledged as one of the Continent's most polluted waterways. The delta area provides refuge for perhaps 100 varieties of fish and upward of 150 bird species. Its drier reaches support substantial populations of wild mammals, including reed wolves that climb trees and a variety of wild dog, *Nyctereutes procynoides,* that originated in China and was brought to Russia to be raised for its fur. The

A Camargue vineyard on land that was once salt marsh is inundated with water pumped from the nearby Rhone River. The fresh water leaches salt from the soil and drowns a destructive insect pest that winters in vine roots.

wild dogs of the Danube delta, presumably descended from animals that escaped from fur farms, were first spotted in 1951.

The impending threat to the incomparable Las Marismas marshes of Spain grows out of their location in the midst of Las Côto de Doñana, a region, including a national park, whose splendid beaches are increasingly popular among European vacationers. At its northwest edge, the park abuts the thriving resort community of Matalascañas, a midsummer mecca for thousands of people from northern Europe. In the earlier years of its development, the resort had a traumatic impact on life in the marshes: Unwary wildfowl alighting too near town frequently graced the menus of local restaurants, and animals living near the margins of the reserve became irresistible prey to unconfined dogs and cats roaming out from the resort. River waters were polluted by the effluents of civilization.

Luckily, the wild creatures of Las Marismas have had friends in high places. There has been considerable international interest in the region since 1957, when some of Europe's most eminent biologists mounted a drive to save this former hunting preserve of Spanish kings and make it the "greatest biological preserve in Europe." The prestigious World Wildlife Fund supported the effort, and a number of prominent European nature lovers joined in the fund-raising appeal. As a result, the Doñana nature reserve and biological research station were established in 1964. The funds also permitted expansion of the national park to include 98,800 additional acres of ornithologically valuable marshland. The park was further protected by special mention in an international treaty for the preservation of wetland areas.

After being diverted into shallow pools at a commercial saltworks along Portugal's Gilao River estuary, sea water evaporates quickly under a hot sun. Workers gather the salt residue with long-handled wooden rakes.

The Taming of England's Fens

The earliest known attempt to tame the wetland wilderness called The Fens in eastern England was made in the First Century A.D. by the occupying forces of Rome. Extending westward from The Wash—a long estuary of the North Sea—the salt marshes and peat bogs of The Fens were scarcely above sea level. This utterly flat area was often flooded by its many shallow, meandering rivers and by high tides that sometimes pushed more than 10 miles upstream from The Wash. The Romans built sea walls along portions of The Wash's shore and dug channels (one may have been more than 60 miles long) to divert water from the sites of their garrisons in The Fens. But after they abandoned England their engineering projects fell into disrepair.

No ambitious effort was made to drain The Fens until the 17th Century, when the Duke of Bedford hired a Dutch engineer named Cornelius Vermuyden to convert the wetlands into agricultural land. Vermuyden straightened the courses of sinuous rivers to increase their velocity and reduce the risk of flooding. A network of small canals was dug to carry water into the reshaped rivers, and sluice gates were installed across their mouths to block the tides. The project was not initially an unqualified success, for as the soggy peat dried, it contracted and subsided by as much as 10 feet, actually making flooding worse in spots. Pumps—first driven by windmills, later by steam, diesel and electricity—overcame this problem.

After three centuries of effort, reclamation of The Fens has yielded 115,000 acres of new land, some of it the most fertile in all of England. Tide-deposited marine silt that was once covered by cord grass and other salt-tolerant plants now supports orchards and fields of wheat, vegetables, tulips and daffodils.

The original seascape of The Fens is preserved on one side of a sea wall, where the salt marsh merges with the estuarine waters of The Wash. On the other side, productive fields have replaced the marshland.

Were it not for its protected status, Las Marismas might well have become all but extinct. But the marsh also has qualities of its own that sustain it against the onslaught of civilization. Foremost among these is its inexorable seasonal transformation from an immense sea of still water created by winter flooding, in which the only landforms are transitory islets, to a parched wilderness of cracked earth stretching endlessly over thousands of acres in high summer.

This annual cycle begins with the winter rains. The Guadalquivir River, bearing salt-laden tidal water from the Gulf of Cádiz at its mouth, overflows its banks and floods Las Marismas. All but the high marsh, elevated strips of land, the interior salt-water mud flats and northerly fresh-water mud flats, are inundated. Meanwhile, seeds of marsh sedge and grasswort provide food for thousands of ducks and wild geese returning from their summer homes in Scandinavia. By mid-December these flocks will constitute one of the largest populations of aquatic birds in the world.

With the coming of spring, the burning Spanish sun begins to make its mark. Evaporation sets in, and the still water becomes shallower, subsiding into a thick tangle of marsh grasses. Before a month has passed, the sedges, galingale and other grasses have become an impenetrable jungle. Within it, suspended on the tall reeds, perched on clumps of mud, floating on the shallow water, are hidden thousands upon thousands of nests: The marsh has become Europe's greatest bird-breeding ground. Black-necked grebes, little bitterns, coots, reed warblers, purple herons, egrets, black-winged stilts and numerous other species are everywhere, feeding, flying about in search of food, resting, nurturing their young. Big-horned marsh cattle and agile fallow deer graze in the thick grasses; pink flamingos blanket the salt lagoons, their exotic plumage mirrored in the shallow water.

Throughout the spring the water level falls lower and lower. By June the quiet lagoons and marshy coves have become hot, muddy quagmires. The birds leave Las Côto de Doñana in search of more hospitable regions farther inland. The exodus is completed by July; by August death and drought haunt a desert that was so recently a fertile marsh. The fiery sun rides high in the sky, and the carcasses of unwary cattle and deer blacken under its merciless rays. As one witness to this bizarre transformation has written, the Doñana marsh is "a colossus which does not permit half measures. Life and death succeed each other inexorably, without mitigation."

The coastal wetlands of the United States are no less threatened by advancing urbanization than are those of Europe. Indeed, American disregard—if not downright dislike—of tide marshes traces back to Colonial times, when port-city residents began filling them in to accommodate wharves, warehouses and housing. The attitude became policy in 1850, when Congress passed the Swamp Land Act to encourage the reclamation of wetlands through diking, draining and filling. Since then, about half of the total wetland acreage along the United States coast has been dried out and converted to so-called productive uses.

The advent of urban planning, with its emphasis on garbage-fill technology and industrial-park development, contributed heavily to the destruction of coastal wetlands. Local governments, eager to increase their tax base—particularly if it meant getting rid of some mosquitoes in the bargain—were generally eager to approve new projects that would turn soggy marshes into dry land. By the 1970s wetlands were disappearing at a rate of some 300,000 acres per year. Marshes were drained and dredged to create marinas, and filled and paved for airport runways. The gigantic sports complex in the New Jersey Meadowlands, just across the George Washington Bridge from uptown Manhattan, was built in the 1970s on top of a rich Hackensack River tide marsh. The former nesting place of more than 200 bird species became the site of a stadium, arena and race track.

Over the past quarter century or so, however, ecologists and biologists have come to recognize the importance of wetlands as habitats and food producers. Such recognition has hardly halted the wholesale destruction of the nation's tidal marshes, but it has had at least one beneficial effect. Under pressure from environmentalists, the U.S. Army Corps of Engineers, which is largely responsible for maintaining waterways and coastlines, has discovered that new tide marshes can be built from scratch. Dredged silt is pulled up by a drag bucket and dumped and spread to raise the bottom level of an inshore area to a point high enough for seeding with marsh vegetation. It is also possible, by planing down, bulldozing or removing old garbage dumps or landfills, to resuscitate marsh areas that have been smothered. In recent years, these restorative capabilities have led to the conservation practice known as mitigation, under which tidal wetlands cannot be filled in legally unless there is an agreement to restore a comparable area to tide-marsh status.

There have been a number of mitigation projects in San Francisco Bay. In one, a 50-acre expanse of shoreline inside the mouth of the Napa River was restored to marshland in exchange for permitting the city of Vallejo to fill an 11-acre tract along the Mare Island strait and use it as an industrial site. The largest example of mitigation on the Pacific coast was the restoration of a 210-acre marsh expanse that had been used since 1948 by the city of Hayward, California, as a garbage dump. Here, the state government agreed to bear more than half the costs in partial restitution for wetlands that were ruined during the construction of a bridge across the southern portion of San Francisco Bay.

Some marine scientists have their doubts about mitigation, viewing it as a possible rationale for continued obliteration of marshes and other wetlands near urban areas, with the substitution of "instant" marshes in more remote locations. An additional objection is that mitigation could wipe out other seashore features that are just as ecologically valuable as salt marshes. In regions such as the northwestern United States, for example, there are no coastal marshes like those found in California and along the Atlantic and Gulf coasts. "In order to build marshes here," Oregon State University's Jefferson Gonor observes, "you just about have to destroy tide flats, and it's a very bad exchange."

Scientists may argue about the relative merits of mitigation and preservation, but they welcome the growing concern about the fate of the world's wetlands. And all would agree with the director of Spain's Las Côto de Doñana nature reserve, who observed in the 1970s, as preservation of the wetland wilderness entrusted to his care was growing more difficult: "People say, what does it matter—a few ducks having a hard time? I say to them it does matter. Because all life is related, all things are connected. The fact that we are human beings does not mean that we are separate from the other living things on this planet." Ω

MARVELS OF LAS MARISMAS

Covering [ ] uare miles of south-western S[ ] the forbidding marshes known as L[ ] Marismas are locked in a harsh cycle of flooding and drought that converts the[ ] from a shallow lake at one time of yea[ ] to a salt desert at another. Yet this rem[ ]te region, where the Guadalquivir River meets the Gulf of Cádiz, shelters a variety of migrant birds and other wild creatures that is unequaled in any o[ ] erness area of Europe.

A [ ] ain's Doñana National Park, [ ] ge of rich alluvial soil is inundated each winter by heavy rains and floodwaters that overflow the many channels of the lower Guadalquivir. At their high point in winter, the floodwaters, bracki[ ] from the frequent incursions of th[ ] alt tides up the estuary, cover most[ ] the marsh to a depth of a foot or two[ ] n spring, luxuriant vegetation rises above the receding waters.

Marsh grasses, along with the insects and aquati[ ] ife that flourish among them, offe[ ] most limitless sustenance to the 200[ ] more bird species that migrate from Africa and elsewhere in Euro[ ] o nest in Las Marismas. Astonished at the avian abundance during a visit to the marshes in the 1890s, British naturalist Abel Chapman wrote, "Imagination can hardly picture, nor Nature provide, a region more congenial to the tastes of wild aquatic birds."

During the wet season, the larger animals inhabiting the stretch of dunes and savanna that divides Las Marismas from the sea share in the marsh's riches. Deer and wild boar forage among the lush vegetation, while lynx stalk well-fattened waterfowl and rabbits.

In the parched months of late summer and fall, most of the birds depart and the marshes dry out, their vegetation withering in the heat. Only the creatures of the marsh fringe remain—a kind of guardian populace that will see this extraordinary coastal realm through the bleak months until the winter rains return and the cycle begins anew.

Spiked with reeds and clotted with algae, brackish floodwaters from the winter inundation still cover Las Marismas in early spring. The waters will persist into May, slowly receding beneath a thickening carpet of verdure.

A black-winged stilt displays the legs for which it is named. This shore bird's stature and rapier bill adapt it to feeding in the flooded marshes, where it plucks small aquatic creatures from the water.

A squacco heron perches on its nest while its mate roosts above. Herons representing most European species nest side by side in breeding grounds around the edge of the marshes, attracted by the seclusion and the ample supply of insects and fish.

Gathering for their late-summer migration, storks festoon a dead cork oak on the fringe of the marshes. The storks will winter as far south as South Africa, then return to Europe to nest.

Pratincoles patrol an island of permanently dry land in the marshes. These insect-eating shore birds nest on the bare ground in regions where saline soil restricts vegetation growth.

A lynx prowls the fertile grasslands bordering the marshes. Hunted almost to extinction in the rest of southern Europe, the 50-pound cats abound in the Doñana wildlife preserve, where they stalk rabbits, birds and fawns.

Fallow deer forage in the drying marsh of autumn. The abundance of deer and wild boar in the Doñana region attracted hunting parties of Spanish royalty as early as the 13th Century.

A mongoose surveys its scrub domain. The rabbits and other small mammals that populate the fringe of the marsh make up its principal diet, along with an occasional poisonous viper.

A sere mosaic under the late-summer sun,
the parched surface of Las Marismas conceals
seeds and underground stems that will
sprout into next year's luxuriance when rain and
floodwaters again drown the marshes.

Chapter 5

THE STRUGGLE TO STOP THE SEA

As the morning fog over the broad Italian lagoon begins to lift, the outlines of smokestacks, storage tanks and refineries loom slowly into view along the tidelands of the shore. Then, out in the middle of the lagoon, a gauzy apparition begins to materialize—a golden island city, the domes and bell towers of its splendid palaces shimmering in the low morning light. This is Venice, the dowager of the Adriatic.

From its singular location in a small pocket of the sea, Venice has extended its influence over much of the world for 1,500 years. Venetian ships, built at the rate of one a day during the city's glory years as an independent republic, controlled immensely profitable trade routes linking jewel- and spice-rich Byzantium with luxury-loving Europe. Venice grew unimaginably rich, yet it rested secure from the threat of invading armies. Access to the encircling lagoon could be readily restrained, and the lagoon itself was laced with mud flats that could serve as a further deterrent: In 1379, when Genoa launched the only invasion of the republic ever attempted, the Venetians yanked up all the navigation signs and channel markers in the lagoon, leaving the Genoese fleet to founder in the muck. Nor have defense and trade been the only gifts of the sea. The twice-daily tides coursing through the city's 160 canals have functioned as an efficient, self-flushing sewage system.

But the Adriatic Sea, which for so long has blessed and protected Venice, now appears bent on reclaiming it. Weighted down by the densely built city, the land beneath Venice has sunk about nine inches in the last 100 years. At the same time, the melting of the polar ice sheets is contributing to a steady global rise in sea level. In addition, artesian wells have depleted the city's underground water supply, or aquifer, and accelerated the sinking process. Each year, the line of green algae that marks the high-water line creeps upward on walls, posts and columns. And the city's canals are overflowing with increasing frequency; in 1919, high tides inundated St. Mark's Square, site of one of the best-loved churches of Christendom, 28 times. In 1981, the square was flooded 60 times. "The walls are falling apart as if they were made of sugar," laments the custodian of the 900-year-old structure. "There's no time for the basilica to dry out now before it's wet again."

Venice's peril is by no means unique. Floods are a deadly threat in the Netherlands, where half the population lives below sea level. Southern England and, in the United States, the Mississippi River delta, the Galveston Bay area of Texas and Long Beach, California, have all experienced

Mirrored by a skim of water, a businessman strides along a duckwalk across St. Mark's Square in Venice. A storm caused this flooding, but many parts of the ancient island city, which has been sinking for 1,000 years, are similarly beset at each high tide.

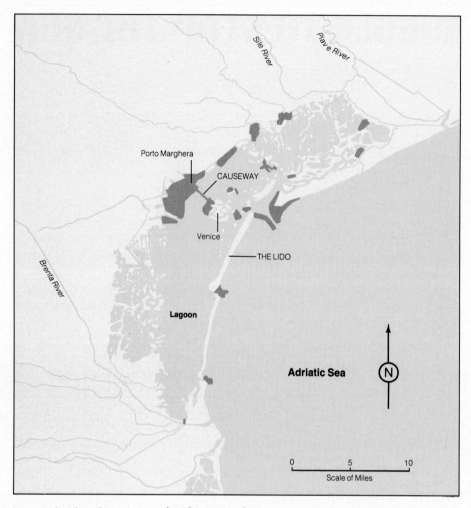

Partially shielded behind a nine-mile strip of barrier islands, Venice lies in a 210-square-mile lagoon. The city is linked by a causeway to the Italian mainland—and to industrial regions built on coastal landfill *(green)*.

increasingly alarming subsidence and consequent danger from the sea.

The responses to the hazard have been varied. In the Netherlands, a significant portion of the national wealth has been committed to expanding and improving the web of dams and dikes that hold the sea at bay. In the face of a far lesser degree of danger, a multimillion-dollar floodgate system has been erected in the Thames River to protect London. Yet in Venice, despite the real possibility that the city's cultural treasures—priceless frescoes and friezes by Tintoretto and Titian, glorious panels by Veronese, and Byzantine and Renaissance churches and palaces—may be lost to the encroaching lagoon, bureaucratic discord has slowed the emplacement of protective measures.

Venice is not one island but 118 islets spliced together by some 400 bridges. About 15,000 years ago, during the last period of glaciation, the northern end of the present-day Adriatic Sea was dry. A fresh-water lake existed where the Venice lagoon is now, with a delta formed by the outlets of several small rivers. As the glaciers melted and the sea rose, the lake was transformed into a brackish lagoon dotted with muddy islands. About two millennia ago, a sandspit barrier now known as the Lido formed at the seaward edge of the lagoon, shielding the islands from the open sea.

When ravaging Visigoths, Lombards and Ostrogoths swarmed over Italy in the Sixth Century, the people of the delta region fled to the safety of the islands. Noting the invaders' lack of nautical skill, the refugees elected to settle there permanently. To build shelters on the difficult terrain, they sank larch pilings through the mud and into the clay substrata, then erected houses and other structures on them. They obtained fresh water by digging wells down through the islands into the substrata below the lagoon. As the community became a trading and shipbuilding center, dredging and filling techniques were devised to consolidate some areas; others were linked by a system of canals and bridges.

To a remarkable extent, the early Venetians seem to have understood the physical processes of the lagoon ecosystem—the cleansing and nutritional functions of the tides and the flood protection offered by the mud flats, called *barene,* that dispersed the high tides. During the heyday of the Venetian republic, an official known as the superintendent of the waters wielded immense authority, second only to that of the ruling doge. He could dictate restrictions on sewage and garbage disposal and on the dredging, filling and navigation of waterways. These were heavy responsibilities; at the investiture of the superintendent, the doge would admonish the citizenry, "Weigh him, pay him, and if he fails, hang him."

Venice's enterprising merchants opened trade routes southward to North Africa and as far north as Flanders and England. The republic's military men were also busy; in the 13th Century, Venice captured a portion of the moribund Byzantine Empire and collected an astonishing booty of wealth and artistic treasures. Venetians came to acquire, as art historian Bernard Berenson noted, "a love of comfort, of ease and of splendor, a refinement of manner and humaneness of feeling which made them the first really modern people of Europe."

Nature, however, often seemed to conspire against their comfort and well-being. Rivers draining into the lagoon deposited silt, building up the mud flats until they encroached on shipping channels and choked the fishing grounds in the shallows. Major floods occurred in every lifetime. When the strong fall and winter winds off the North African desert coincided with unusually high tides, they pushed water up into the northern end of the Adriatic and into the Venice lagoon. These winds—the sirocco—sometimes brought catastrophic damage and death, for there was no high ground to which Venetians could retreat.

A threat of a very different sort arose in the second half of the 15th Century. The successful voyage of the Portuguese navigator Vasco da Gama around the African continent to India spelled the end of Venice's dominance of trade with the East; European merchants no longer had to pass through Venice on their way to the Black Sea and the terminals of the overland trade routes to Asia. By the end of the 16th Century, Venetian trade had dwindled by half.

But Venice showed itself to be resilient. The city's traders responded to the dearth of Far Eastern imports by taking up the export business and offering for sale the products of their own area's craftsmen. Stonecutters, glass blowers, printers, weavers and engravers, attracted by the demand for their crafts and by the existence of strong artisan guilds in Venice, began to flock to the city to live and work. Prosperous families displayed their wealth by building elaborate villas and palaces ornamented with the work of resident artists. Under the sponsorship of the merchant families, Venetian painters produced art in astounding quantity—literally acres of it—for the walls and ceilings of churches, palaces and public buildings. Shiploads of marble were imported and chiseled into statuary, reliefs and the ornate fretwork that would be the hallmark of the Venetian façade. Unfortunately, the lagoon city was growing not just more beautiful but, as stone replaced wood, much heavier.

Although Venetians could not sense that their city was sinking, they were well aware of the problem of siltation in the lagoon. In 1550, nearly a century after the proposal was first made, a gifted and persuasive hydrographer named Cristoforo Sabbadino was able to win backing for a project to divert the silt-laden rivers draining into the lagoon and thus prevent the blockage of the Adriatic tides. In his most telling argument, Sabbadino likened the tidal action in the lagoon to the respiratory process: The marshes and mud flats allowed the lagoon to expand like a lung to be renewed and refreshed; siltation constricted these tidal margins and suffocated the lagoon. His reasoning was sound, but the massive project, which took more than a century to complete, would have unforeseen and far-reaching consequences.

Protecting the *barene* from sedimentation had no effect, of course, on the continuing rise of the sea level or the recurrent siroccos that blew great tides into the lagoon. In mid-December of 1600, a disastrous *acqua alta,* or high tide, broke through the Lido at several points and inundated the city. A resident wrote of the scene: "Roaring horribly, the sea rose up toward the sky, causing a terrible fear through the whole of Venice." Damage was later estimated at more than a million gold pieces.

As relentlessly as the tides rose, the fortunes of Venice fell. Faster, more maneuverable ships were being built in northern Europe, and Venice's shipbuilders all but shut down. In 1797, Napoleon seized control of the almost bankrupt republic; in the same year he gave Venice to Austria in return for Belgium, Milan and the left bank of the Rhine. Austrian occupation lasted for 69 years, during which time a causeway was built to connect Venice to the mainland. In 1866, Austria finally abandoned Venice to the kingdom of Italy. By this time it was well known that Venice was sinking. Lord Byron, who spent years exploring the city's narrow alleyways, mourned, "Oh Venice! When thy marble walls / Are level with the water, there shall be / A cry of nations o'er thy sunken halls, / A loud lament along the sweeping sea!"

But aside from inspiring melancholy poetry, the threat of the rising waters did not stimulate any countermeasures until the reemergence of Venice as an industrial center after World War I. The nadir of Venice's commercial fortunes was reached in the midst of that war with the closing of a once-mighty arsenal where warships and armaments were made. Eight thousand Venetians lost their jobs, and the city was left without a major industry. A coalition of leading Venetian families decided that the key to recovery was the development of an industrial complex on land that would be reclaimed by filling in the *barene* at the edge of the Venice lagoon.

Porto Marghera, as it came to be called, was built on more than 1,200 acres of landfill near the mainland end of the causeway. It met with considerable success, and beginning in 1950 another 1,235 acres of *barene* and nearly twice that expanse of adjacent countryside were cleared for industrial expansion. The three historic inlets to the lagoon, at Lido, Malomocco and Chioggia, were expanded and dredged to three times their previous

A dense canopy of red tile roofs obscures the cluster of 118 islands on which Venice is built. The weight of the compact city has contributed to the sinking of the land beneath it and thus to the ever more frequent flooding.

The rising lagoon that surrounds Venice leaves its signature, a line of green algae, on the façade of a once-stately home. Many families have abandoned the first floors of their houses because of incursions of the tides.

depth to permit entry of larger ships, and a canal was cut in the harbor to permit oil tankers to enter the lagoon. Greater Venice was once again a major Italian port.

But Venetians soon had reason to recall Sabbadino's 16th Century warnings against impeding the lagoon's "respiratory" functions. Pollutants became more concentrated in the lagoon. Furthermore, the expanded channels of the three inlets enabled the tides to enter the lagoon at a much faster rate than before, and the industrial development had reduced by nearly one third the area of marshes and mud flats available to accommodate the water; the high tides became higher than ever. Conversely, as the tide ebbed, the water went out much faster, emptying the lagoon to an appreciably lower level than before. The latter phenomenon is especially destructive. Such supports as wooden pilings and stone or brick walls last for centuries when always submerged or always dry; but when long submerged and then exposed to drying, they will split or rot.

Another consequence of the industrial expansion that had not been widely foreseen was an acceleration of the subsidence of the lagoon floor and of Venice itself. Historically, the lagoon area had been amply supplied with fresh water from a generous aquifer. As the new industries drew copiously from the aquifer, this underground water supply became depleted; the land above it, deprived of the water's support, sank. Thus the scene was set for disaster.

It came on November 3, 1966. Gale-force winds bearing heavy rains had blown up from the Mediterranean, and Venetians, from long habit, fortified their homes and businesses in anticipation of a severe *acqua alta*. The evening tide reached its peak at 10 p.m. Then, instead of ebbing, it stayed, held inside the lagoon by the force of the southeast gale. At 5 a.m., when the tide should have been low, the water level still had not dropped. By noon the next day, a second high tide had pushed the waters over the canal banks and deep into St. Mark's Square. Again that evening the tide did not go out but continued to rise, reaching 6½ feet above normal high water; waves broke high on the columns and arches of the Renaissance-era Ducal Palace. When the gale finally eased late on the night of November 4, the water rushed out of the lagoon, leaving a ghastly shroud of sludge, sewage, oil and filth in its wake. Damage to the city's ships, homes, churches and museums seemed beyond calculation; eventually it was estimated at six billion dollars.

Historians and art lovers around the world quickly raised money to finance the restoration of the city's damaged art and architecture. In addition, the devastation energized a quest for solutions to the long-term problems that promised even worse future flooding. The Italian government established a scientific survey group, assigned to it the weighty title of the Institute for the Study of the Dynamics of Grand Masses and appointed a distinguished Italian scientist named Roberto Frassetto to chair it.

Engineers test an experimental water-filled rubber dam in a small channel in the Venetian lagoon. As conceived, the barrier could be deflated to permit the transit of ships through the channel during normal tides.

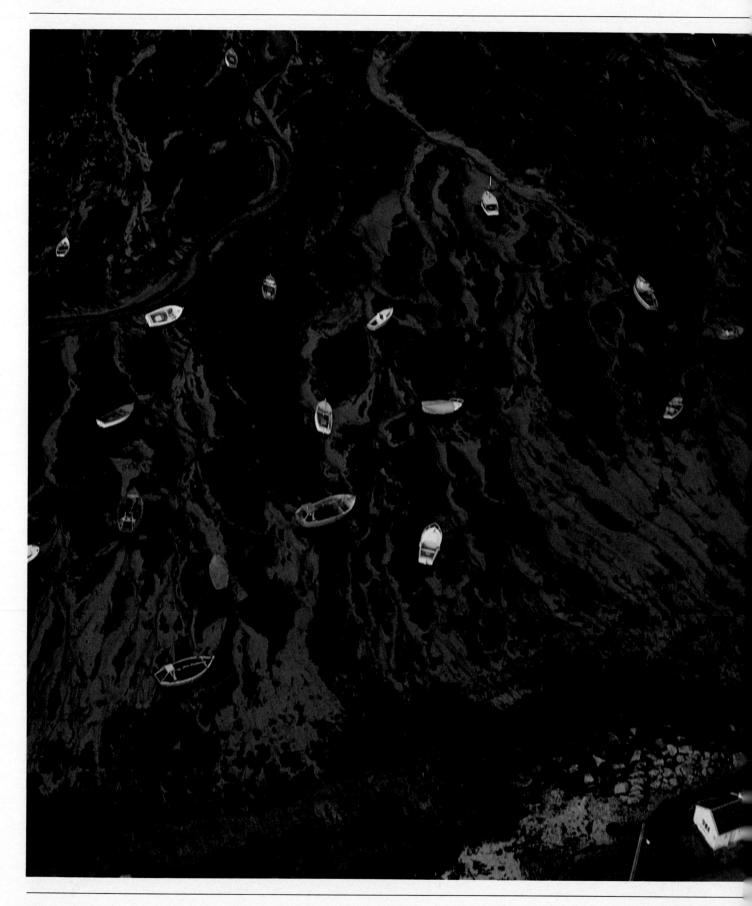

The Black Death of the "Amoco Cadiz"

The use of enormous supertankers to transport oil has raised a new threat to coastlines. Every year, approximately 150,000 tons of oil are spilled into the world's oceans as a result of shipping accidents. The majority of these spills take place in the hazardous shallows close to the shore.

The damage that can be done by the wreck of a supertanker was memorably demonstrated in March of 1978, when the supertanker *Amoco Cadiz* broke her steering gear and drifted toward the coast of Brittany. Her SOS was answered quickly by a German tug, but the two captains haggled for three hours over the cost of a tow as a gathering storm buffeted the crippled tanker. By the time the terms were finally arranged, the wind had built to a velocity of more than 35 miles per hour. The rescue attempt failed, and the *Amoco Cadiz* had to be abandoned. Fifteen-foot seas smashed the ship against nearby rocks and broke her apart, releasing 223,000 tons of crude oil into the water.

Spread rapidly by the wind, the oil formed a scum 60 miles long and up to 12 miles wide. The black tide despoiled 72 miles of coast, staining the granite cliffs and seeping two feet into the white-sand beaches. It smothered oyster, lobster and mussel beds, wiped out seaweed farms and suffocated an estimated 48,000 birds.

French soldiers and volunteer workers shoveled up enough of the oily sludge along the beaches to fill 17,700 railroad boxcars, but its effects would remain for a decade. A damage estimate of $300 million did not include the losses sustained by fishermen, by farmers whose crops were contaminated by oily sea spray or by those employed in tourist-related businesses.

The black film of oil from the breakup of the supertanker *Amoco Cadiz* surrounds a French fishing fleet. In all, the thick scum covered 400 square miles of the Atlantic.

Yellow-jacketed volunteers work to remove the sludge that befouled miles of the intertidal region along Brittany's coast following the 1978 oil spill. Despite such efforts, hundreds of species of shore-dwelling life were decimated.

Frassetto and his staff first collected detailed information about the mechanics of recent disasters—water levels and velocities, atmospheric pressures, wind speeds and direction. Using a computer programed with a mathematical model of the lagoon, the researchers analyzed the effect of various circumstances on the water level in the lagoon; soon they were able to devise a method for predicting when any combination of factors would produce a flood in Venice. The system would prove its effectiveness in November of 1975 by providing six hours' warning of impending floods.

The overriding concern of the Institute, however, was to find a way to protect the lagoon from flood tides without interfering with the passage of ships during good weather. An international competition was held to stimulate ideas. One intriguing response was a proposal to lay an enormous rubber tube across the floor of each one of the lagoon entrances. Deflated, the tubes would allow free passage of ships and water above them. When a flood threatened, pumps would fill the tubes with water, causing them to swell upward into a fairly rigid barrier at the entrances. Frassetto and the Institute endorsed the idea of such a flexible system because its ecological consequences were minor. But the Italian Public Works Ministry decided in favor of a different approach—a permanent narrowing of the lagoon entrances.

The hotly argued difference of opinion stymied any action until 1982, when $6.5 million was appropriated to study a barrier design that was a sort of compromise between the flexibility advocated by the Institute and the permanence sought by the Ministry. This plan envisioned a row of steel cylinders, each about 16 feet in diameter, anchored in a concrete base across the floor of each inlet. Hinged at their bases, the cylinders would lie on the floor of the lagoon, permitting ships to pass above them, until a flood tide threatened. Then they would be pumped full of compressed air and would float upward to an angle of about 60 degrees, temporarily sealing the inlets.

On another front, the Institute had already determined that depletion of the fresh-water aquifer under the lagoon quadrupled the subsidence of the lagoon during the 20th Century. This finding resulted in a gradually imposed ban on the use of wells in Venice. Industrial users were forbidden to draw water from the wells in the early 1970s, and city residents were later required to get their fresh water from an aqueduct built in the late 1970s to pipe water from the Alps, almost 100 miles away. The ban had an unexpected and dramatic result; the land not only stopped subsiding but rebounded slightly.

Still, the city's situation remains precarious. Despite the brief rebound due to the ban on depletion of the aquifer, both the natural subsidence of the land and the rise of the seas can be expected to continue. Until a barrier against the tides is in place, St. Mark's Square will be flooded each time the tidal rise exceeds 30 inches.

Perhaps the saddest outcome of all this is that while Rome fiddled, many Venetians, tired of waiting for solutions, packed up and left. Increasing numbers of young people and middle-class workers have taken leave of family heritage and the drafty, damp magnificence of Venice for centrally heated apartments across the causeway. In 1950, about 180,000 Venetians lived on the island; by the early 1980s, fewer than 90,000 remained. Of the cadre of shopkeepers, guides, custodians, gondoliers and restorers who keep the historic center open and accessible to tourists and scholars, more than 20,000 commute to work from homes on the mainland.

However Italy finally acts to forestall the destruction of Venice, neither the threat nor the response can approach in magnitude those in place about 500 miles away in the Netherlands, where an entire nation is at hazard. The welfare—indeed, the survival—of seven million people depends on the integrity of the enormous network of dams and dikes that confronts the sea. All too often in the history of the Low Countries, that web has broken.

Not long after midnight on February 2, 1953, the insistent clang of a fisherman's hand bell sounded an alert in the small Dutch fishing community of Colijnsplaat. It was quickly echoed by the toll of a church bell. Villagers leaped from their beds in response to the alarm, which told them the North Sea was on the rampage again.

The wind had been howling for hours by nightfall on February 1, whipping the sea into a frenzy, smashing enormous waves against a 355-year-old dike. On inspection earlier that evening, the barrier, a stone wall buttressed with brick pillars, had seemed secure enough; the dike master ordered it sandbagged and sent for additional wood and steel beams that might be needed for reinforcement. "At first we did not realize what was happening," a villager said later. "We started to save the household goods in a flooded house." Then a sentinel posted near the dike cried out, "She's giving way!"

The pounding waves had wrested a corner pillar from its foundation. With one more powerful surge, the sea could snap the barricade and roar through to inundate the village and thousands of acres of valuable farmland. Several men rushed to throw their weight against the threatened pillar. Others followed, pushing against the straining bodies in front of them while bone-chilling waves broke over their heads. For two hours, until the reinforcement beams could be brought up and put in place, 40 men formed a living dike and held back the most destructive North Sea storm in 500 years.

Elsewhere that night, the battle against the sea was lost more often than it was won. Hundreds of dikes crumbled before the water. Families awakened by the ringing bells found themselves neck-deep in icy water before they could dress. In some places, water rose 16 feet in 15 minutes, drowning people in their beds. At Gravendeel, near Rotterdam, 600 men, women and children huddling atop a dike were swept away by a gigantic wave of water unleashed by breaking dikes nearby. In the days that followed, helicopters airlifted to safety 2,450 people who had clung in terror to roofs, treetops and telephone poles. Drowning and exposure killed more than 1,800 people. The sea flooded 800,000 acres and ravaged 47,300 homes, thousands of them beyond repair.

During the next nine months, the Dutch closed hundreds of breaches in their fragile bulwark of dikes and began the work of leaching the salt from their farmland. It was of little comfort to know that the storm had been a quirk, a freakish alliance of gale winds and spring tides that is statistically probable only once in 400 years.

Appalling destruction by storms—whether abetted by the tides or not—is a very old story for the Dutch. In the year 1287, a violent storm drove the sea through the earthen dikes and drowned some 50,000 people. In 1421, the sea obliterated 72 villages and in a single night drowned 10

Wind-driven waters of the North Sea pour through breaches in a dike in southern Zeeland and crash against sea walls in Harlingen (*inset*) during a devastating storm that struck the Netherlands on February 1, 1953.

per cent of the population. Rarely has a century since passed without a comparable tragedy. After the devastation of 1953, however, the Dutch were determined to apply technology and engineering on an unprecedented scale to thwart their ancient enemy once and for all.

Like Venice, the Netherlands faces the twin threats of slowly sinking land and steadily rising sea. But more than one quarter of its land—which, with its 14 million inhabitants, is the most densely populated region in Europe—already lies well below sea level (as much as 22 feet). Nearly two million acres of that land has been wrested from the sea by a system of dikes stretching for 1,800 miles.

The geographical basis for the present-day Netherlands was a swampy delta plain at the mouth of the Rhine, Maas and Scheldt Rivers. Superb fishing along the dunes and among the islands of the delta region attracted the earliest settlers, the Frisians, about 450 B.C. In an effort to protect their settlements from floods, they built dirt hillocks, called terpen, to which they could retreat when the water was high. Their accommodation to such inhospitable land astounded Roman soldiers who occupied the area at the outset of the Christian era. Pliny the Elder, stationed with the army, wrote: "Here a miserable people live on high hills or mounds that they have made and on which they have built their huts. They are like sailors when the tide is high and like castaways when the waters have again retreated."

Beginning in the 12th Century, terpen were linked to form dikes. Communities sprang up behind these barriers, knit together by the need to maintain the dikes. Each man was responsible for the stretch of dike that lay on his land, and according to early law, a man who failed to repair a broken dike faced a particularly horrible death; he was to be buried alive in the breach.

A marvelous new weapon in the battle against the sea—the windmill—was introduced into the Low Countries by Christian soldiers returning from the Crusades. This beguiling implement, probably invented by Arabs to irrigate their fields, soon became emblematic of Holland. With windmills to drive their pumps, the Dutch could reclaim vast regions of swampland by surrounding an area with dikes and then pumping out the water; the area thus drained was known as a polder. By 1500, the Dutch were reclaiming land at the rate of almost 300 square miles per century. Nonetheless, floods tore through the dikes so often and engulfed so much land that, despite their efforts, the Dutch barely maintained parity with the sea.

Polderizing took on a new impetus during the 17th Century, a time known as Holland's Golden Age. The Dutch East and West India Companies, trading on every continent, brought enormous wealth back to their homeland. Prosperous Dutch businessmen, always alert to new sources of profit, perceived one in the wealth of small lakes that dotted the countryside; they bought the lakes cheaply, encircled them with dikes, then pumped them dry and sold the much-needed farmland at a healthy markup. The engineer for a number of these projects was a carpenter's son named Jan Adriaanszoon Leeghwater, who had accelerated the draining process by designing a system of windmills that greatly improved pumping capacity. Leeghwater directed the largest reclamation project that had been undertaken up until that time, the draining of the 17,500-acre Beemster Polder with 40 windmills.

His lifelong dream, however, was to drain the Haarlemmermeer, a

A map details the number and extent of the remarkable engineering feats with which the people of the Netherlands protect their country from the North Sea. The dam network (*red*) holds off the tides, provides needed fresh-water reservoirs and offers a measure of security for the Lowlands (*light green*) that have been drained and reclaimed from the sea.

44,500-acre region of lakes and swamps southwest of Amsterdam. The Dutch referred to the area as the Water Wolf, because of the way its ravenous waters gnawed at land and buildings. Leeghwater calculated that 160 windmills would be needed to drain such an extensive area. The Dutch government found the proposal too ambitious and too expensive, and other critics claimed the plan might backfire, causing floods or, by changing the water table, even droughts. More than 200 years after Leeghwater's death, the invention of the steam engine made possible the fulfillment of his vision. Steam-driven pumps labored for three years and three months, until in 1852 the Haarlemmermeer was at last dry land; the Water Wolf had been vanquished. (In the midst of the Haarlemmermeer Polder today, Schiphol, Amsterdam's airport, sprawls on land where Spanish ships were repelled by the Dutch Navy in 1573.) The remarkable engineering achievement caused an admiring Frenchman to remark, "God made the earth, but the Dutch made Holland."

At the end of the 19th Century, the Dutch set their sights even higher, devising a scheme to undo one of the sea's major victories. In a series of dramatic encroachments during the 13th Century (including the devastating flood of 1287), the North Sea had punched through to the country's largest fresh-water lake. Thus was born the Zuider Zee, and virtually overnight the small lakeside fishing village of Amstel was transformed into the seaport now known as Amsterdam. As the population of the Netherlands grew and arable land brought an ever-higher premium, the Dutch thought longingly of the thousands of acres submerged by the Zuider Zee. Many proposals were made to reclaim them, but the feats of engineering required to seal off a 1,500-square-mile sea seemed to be beyond the realm of possibility. Then Cornelius Lely appeared on the scene.

The seventh son of an Amsterdam businessman, Lely pursued an undistinguished career as a civil engineer for 11 years before finding his life's work and the mission that would make him a national hero. In 1886, at the age of 32, Lely joined an association of hydraulic engineers committed to damming the Zuider Zee, on whose shores Lely had spent his youth. A year later, Lely became director of technological research, and in this capacity he wrote a series of eight memoranda in which he presented the first workable plan for building the enormous dam required to close off the inland sea and reclaim some of the land it covered.

Lely was a modest man, but he soon demonstrated that he could be tenacious when supporting his cause; perceiving that his plan would need strong political support if it was ever to be implemented, he embarked on a political career. In 1891, when he was appointed Minister for Waterworks, he named a commission of influential citizens to study his proposal. After two years of analysis, the committee unanimously endorsed the concept.

Elsewhere, however, approval was far from unanimous. Critics maintained that the challenge of building a dam across 22 miles of sea floor against powerful and turbulent tidal currents was far too daunting to undertake, even for a people as experienced in these matters as the Dutch. The plan lay dormant, but Lely persevered, building political connections as he served in Parliament, as governor of the Dutch colony of Surinam in South America, as senator and again as waterworks minister. When he was offered the waterworks post for a third time in 1913, he accepted on condition that the Zuider Zee plan be adopted as policy by the new Cabinet. After a severe food shortage during World War I and disastrous flooding along the shores of the Zee in 1916, the Parliament finally accepted the plan in 1918. The work began the next year. Lely was named President of the Zuider Zee Council and put in charge of the construction.

The project followed, almost to the letter, the eight memoranda Lely had written 40 years earlier. The barrier was built in two parts, a short, two-mile section from the coast of Holland northward to the island of Wieringen in the sea-torn inlet to the Zuider Zee, and a 19-mile-long dam linking Wieringen with the Frisian coast farther north (map, page 157). Construction of the longer dam, known as the Afsluitdijk, was the ordeal its critics had predicted. The dam had to be built in open sea that ranged in depth from 10 to 100 feet. The engineers could foresee that as construction proceeded and the inlet was narrowed, the twice-daily tides would be funneled through an ever-smaller opening, causing a perilous increase in the already powerful currents.

For a practical solution to the engineering problems, Lely turned to a countryman with unique qualifications—Dr. H. A. Lorentz, winner of the 1902 Nobel Prize for physics. Albert Einstein considered Lorentz to be the greatest thinker he had ever known, and had based his theory of relativity on Lorentz' theoretical groundwork. Lorentz spent two years collecting data on currents and tides, then worked for six years calculating their effects. Meanwhile, the comparatively simple task of linking Wieringen island to North Holland was completed. In 1927, equipped with mathematical and tidal formulas developed by Lorentz, a fleet of more than 500 vessels began work on the larger dam.

Locks to permit the passage of ships, as well as sluice gates to regulate the tides, would be needed before the dam was finished, and these were started immediately. The 25 sluice gates and three locks were built in place, in deep pits that had been diked and drained. Construction of the dam itself began in six shallow areas that had been selected in order to minimize the effect on tidal flow. Barges dumped parallel ridges of dense, water-resistant boulder clay, and enormous suction dredges filled the gap between the clay ridges with sand to form the base of the dam. Meanwhile, in the deepest parts of the inlet, dredges dumped boulder clay on the bottom to reduce the scouring action of the current and to serve as the dam's base there. Mattresses of woven willow branches weighted with stone were laid on top of the clay to keep it from being washed away. More clay, backed by sand on the inland side, completed the core of the dam; a facing of stone and brick was laid to protect the seaward slope from the waves. The finished structure was 300 yards wide at its base and stood 10 feet above the highest expected flood-tide level.

After four years of construction, only two gaps remained to be closed. In the fall of 1931, all efforts, and the attention of the country, were directed to the half-mile gap known as Middelgronden. Tidal currents racing at some 20 feet per second had scoured a 100-foot-deep hole in the sea floor and were carrying away fill material almost as fast as it could be dumped into the breach. For a time it appeared that the sea might triumph after all. To make matters worse, a November storm was heading up the coast toward the Zee. To thwart the scouring current, it was decided to shift fill operations to the inland side of the hole for the final assault. A fleet of 27 dredges, 13 cranes, 60 tugs and 132 barges took part in the effort, and they managed to seal the opening. Closure of the final gap six months later, on May 28, 1932, was greeted with blaring horns, unfurling flags and speeches by public officials; but it was an anticlimax for the work crews, whose most desperate battle had already been won.

The freshening of the inland body of water, now a lake named Ijsselmeer for the Ijssel River, which drains into it, got under way immediately. When the dam was completed, the waters of the Ijsselmeer were about one third as saline as sea water. At each low tide, the sluice gates in the dam were opened to allow brackish water to drain away. Closed at all other times, the gates prevented the tides from replenishing the lake's salt content while fresh river water constantly poured in. A year later, the salinity was halved, and within five years it was negligible.

Long before the dam was completed, the land-hungry Dutch had begun diking and draining the first of the Ijsselmeer polders, a 50,000-acre area known as the Wieringermeer. First, canals were dredged in the sea floor to facilitate future drainage and to provide boats later access to the interior portions of the polder; then the area was surrounded with dikes. In 1929, the polder dikes were closed, and in 1930 the Lely Pumping Stations began removing 440,000 gallons of water per minute. After six months, almost 160 billion gallons of water had been pumped out, and the former sea floor was exposed to the air. At first the mushy soil could not support the weight

Farming Seaweed in the Shallows

If Venice and the Netherlands exemplify how civilization can become locked in mortal combat with the sea, Japan supplies a memorable model of the opposite. There, in shallows not unlike the European sites of conflict, farmers patiently raise annual crops of edible seaweed. The most prized variety is a red alga called nori. Each fall, farmers set bamboo poles — or, in recent years, nets — in sheltered waters. Floating spores of the alga cling to the poles and nets, sprout there and within a few weeks grow into leafy plants.

Until 1949, no one knew where each new generation of spores came from; the nori plants themselves simply wither and die after the winter growing season. That year a British botanist, Kathleen Drew, discovered that the dying plants give off a completely different type of spore that settles on mollusk shells and covers them with a growth so unlike nori that it had previously been thought to be a separate species. In the fall, this growth emits the spores that develop into the leafy alga.

Since this discovery, nori growers have increased their production greatly. Government laboratories now put oyster shells in tanks of seawater to collect spores from chopped nori leaves. The shells become encrusted with the off-season growth, and farmers pay a fee to soak their nets and poles in the tanks to seed them with the new spores, which are then set out in the sea to grow.

The leaves are harvested when they are about eight inches long and then chopped, pressed into thin sheets about seven inches square and dried in the sun. Almost tasteless and with a slight sea odor, nori is used as a garnish for soups or sauces and as a wrapping for fish and other foods. Although it has little nutritional value, it holds an honored place in Japanese cuisine.

Japanese sea farmers drift amid a serene forest of bamboo stalks, set in coastal shallows to grow the seaweed delicacy called nori. The plant clings to the bamboo and to the nets (*inset*) that are used by large-scale growers.

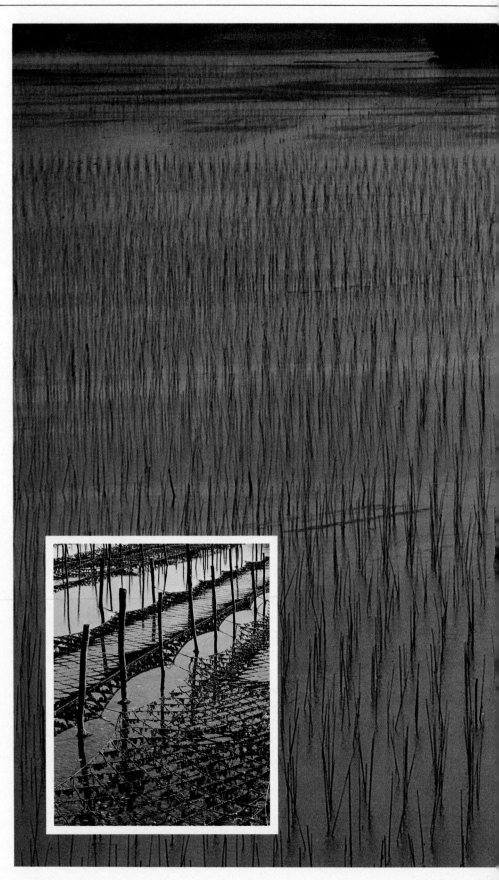

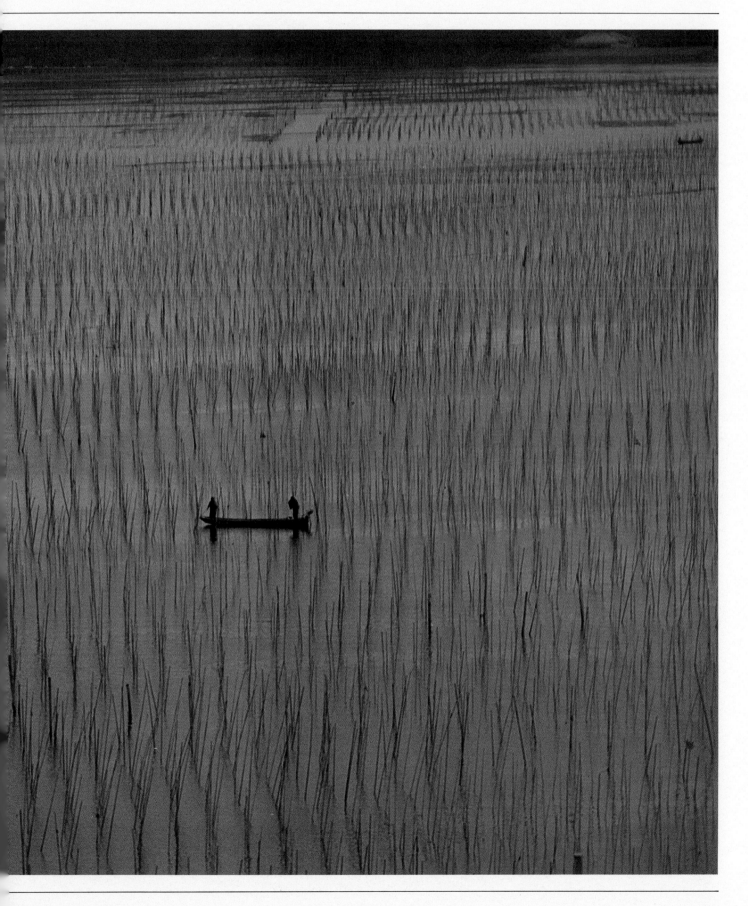

of a person, let alone a machine. Boats moving along the previously excavated canals dredged more ditches to help drain the soil. As the land dried, crops suitable to a saline soil, such as rapeweed and reeds, were sown by hand, plowed under and sown again and again to help stabilize and further dry the soil. By 1941, a total of 511 farms had been established around a nucleus of roads, schools, stores and churches.

Then on April 17, 1945, all that had been gained was suddenly lost. Germany, which had occupied Holland since 1940, dealt the Wieringermeer a vicious blow—one whose motive has never been explained. Perhaps in spiteful fulfillment of an earlier threat that they could return Holland to the 12th Century if they so chose, the occupation troops blasted holes in the

dike and flooded the polder with one billion cubic yards of water. Although no lives were lost, the community was destroyed, with every crop and every tree drowned in salt water. But immediately after the German surrender, the pumps roared to life in the Wieringermeer; a year later, the first crops were sown and rebuilding began, and five years later, in 1950, reconstruction was complete.

By that time the country was enjoying the benefits of its new 300,000-acre lake, an invaluable source of fresh water. The building of the Afsluitdijk had shortened the coastline by 200 miles, which meant the miles of sea dikes that had once restrained the Zuider Zee no longer had to be maintained. With the subsequent diking and draining of three more polders in the lake, the Netherlands increased its land area by almost 5 per cent in a unique and peaceful annexation of territory. What is more, thanks perhaps to the vision of Cornelius Lely and the tidal calculations of Lorentz, the Afsluitdijk withstood the assault of the 1953 storm.

The devastation of that storm was visited on Zeeland, south of Ijsselmeer at the delta formed by arms of the Rhine, Scheldt and Maas Rivers. Three weeks after the storm, the Delta Commission—a group of civil engineers

Practicing an age-old craft, Dutch workers complete a woven mattress of willow branches by adding stone ballast. The mattresses are used as a base for conventional dams to help thwart erosion of the sea floor.

162

A massive rig called the *Cardium* lays down prefabricated mats of nylon and steel—a stronger modern alternative to the traditional willow mattresses—to stabilize the sea floor for construction of the Eastern Scheldt Dam.

and others—was set up to plan the Netherlands' defenses against a recurrence of the disaster. The commission focused on two alternatives: The 434 miles of existing dikes in the delta area could be strengthened and built higher; or an enormous network of barrier dams, much like the successful Afsluitdijk, could be built to seal off the delta's four estuaries from the sea. These barriers would have to be backed up by a system of inland dams, locks and sluices to regulate the outflow of the rivers. The Western Scheldt River, which served as a shipping channel to Antwerp, and the Rotterdam Waterway would remain open and the dikes along their banks would be strengthened.

The second proposal was far from new; long before the Zuider Zee project came to fruition, the Dutch had considered severing the four fingers of salt water that intruded into the delta. Converted to fresh-water lakes, the estuaries would serve as a buffer against the salt water that had been creeping inland and threatening arable land. As their new offensive against the sea, the Delta Commission and the Netherlands Parliament selected the second option, in the form of a proposal first made in 1949 to link the islands of Zeeland to South Holland with four dams, thereby snipping off 440 miles of estuarine coastline. This plan became known as the Delta Project.

No one had ever attempted such an enterprise. It called for 18.5 miles of dams to be anchored on unstable sea floor in water as much as 132 feet deep while the sand shifted and currents raced through the estuarine inlets at 15 feet per second. Delta Project engineers decided to work from the smallest project to the largest in order to gain experience along the way. Computers speeded the calculating of the forces of tides and currents. If done by the pencil-and-paper methods Lorentz had used for Afsluitdijk, the work might have required 25 years; the computers developed the required formulas in three years. Hydrological laboratories built scale models of Zeeland's estuaries by the acre, complete with algae growing along the concrete riverbeds and tiny motors and pumps agitating the water to simulate wave action, tidal motion and even the rotation of the earth.

The overriding question during these years of planning was how high to build the dams. Traditionally, dam and dike heights had been based on previous high-water levels. But in 1953, the sea had risen 12 feet 6 inches higher than had ever been recorded before; taught a bitter lesson, engineers decided to rely instead on mathematical probability. They gathered data on the geological and meteorological forces that contributed to high water and determined that it was possible for a combination of storm and tides to raise the sea 3 feet 11 inches higher than the crest of the 1953 flood. Although such a storm could be expected to happen only once in 10,000 years, they resolved to build the Delta Project dikes to withstand that possibility.

When the plan had been drawn up, there remained the problem of assembling the gargantuan tools needed to implement it. In many cases, no existing equipment was large enough to build, hoist or position the immense prefabricated components required. The Dutch began to innovate on a grand scale, drawing first on technology born of the demands of World War II. To construct artificial harbors rapidly near the beaches where the D-Day invasion took place, Allied engineers had used enormous concrete-and-steel caissons that could be towed into position, then sunk and stabilized with clay ballast. The Dutch adopted the design of the caissons, adding sluice gates, and used them for the first time in the Veerse Gat Dam, completed in 1961.

The caissons, each as big as a city block, were built in shallow-water areas that had been surrounded by cofferdams and pumped dry. When construction was complete, each cofferdam was breached to flood the work area and permit the caissons to be floated for transport. Openings in the sides of the caissons were covered temporarily with wooden doors while the structures were towed to the Veerse Gat channel. Then the wooden doors were removed and the caissons were sunk to the sea floor, where the tides moved unimpeded through them. When all the caissons were in place, the engineers were ready to lock out the sea in one stroke: At a moment of slack water, steel gates were slammed down over the open sides of all the caissons. In this way, the treacherous scouring effect of racing water that nearly sabotaged the Afsluitdijk was avoided. Layers of sand topped with asphalt and concrete completed the dam.

Construction by caisson proved to be slow. Stymied by rough seas and bad weather, crews could only rarely place more than one caisson per day, so the method was best suited for small channels. A much more rapid technique was devised for the broader expanse of the Grevelingen River dam and later used on other dams. A cableway was suspended from towers directly

In a technique designed to speed dam construction, a Dutch cable car prepares to drop a 2½-ton concrete block into place in the spine of the Brouwers Dam. The cars can work around the clock and in any weather.

above the location of the dam. Cable cars could then carry up to 10 tons of concrete blocks at a time to a predetermined position and drop them into place, repeating the process until a spine of concrete blocks rose to the desired height. Unhampered by darkness, weather or current, the cable cars could work 24 hours a day.

Engineers faced very different challenges in designing and building the Haringvliet Dam, which connects the two northernmost islands of Zeeland. Through this three-mile-wide inlet, 60 per cent of the waters of the Rhine and Maas Rivers flowed into the sea. Damming the inlet would have the desirable effect of diverting this discharge northward into the Rotterdam Waterway, where the resulting steady flow of water would prevent siltation that could otherwise threaten the channel serving one of the world's busiest ports. But if the rivers flooded, the excess water would somehow have to be released to the sea, and in winter a way would have to be found to prevent ice from accumulating behind the dam until it choked the waterway.

The response of the Delta Project engineers was a design incorporating 17 pairs of sluice gates. Normally closed, the gates would be capable of opening to discharge flood waters, ice or, during the desalinization process, salt water at low tide. The gates called for would be the largest ever built to that time, wide enough to allow icebreakers to ram through to the sea in winter. Since transporting the gates would present proportionately large problems, an on-site construction method was chosen. First, a cofferdam enclosure almost a mile long was created where the dam would rise. Piers and spans were built in place; then the sluice gates, each 180 feet wide and weighing 425 tons, were fitted onto the piers. With the sluices complete, the encircling dam was dredged away and dams were built spanning the distance from the shore to the sluice complex.

Deep within the dam, engineers included a series of tunnels that allow migratory ocean fish to reach their fresh-water spawning grounds. Windows line the undersea tunnels, so visitors can watch the mysterious migrations that continue unimpeded by the colossus of Haringvliet.

After completion of the Haringvliet in 1971 and the larger but simpler Brouwers Dam in 1972, the Delta Project ground to a halt. Concern had

Legions of 131-foot-tall concrete piers shown below, built for the Netherlands' Eastern Scheldt storm-surge barrier, await transport from their flooded

cofferdam construction pit while work continues on the piers in the dry cofferdam in the background.

spread over the ecological consequences of damming off the last and loveliest of Zeeland's estuaries, the Eastern Scheldt. Environmentalists, commercial fishermen and oyster growers, aware that closure would kill off the highly varied salt-water flora and fauna, lobbied for an open estuary.

In order to appease the environmentalists as well as those who insisted on the flood protection of a dam, the Netherlands government adopted an extremely expensive compromise, a storm-surge barrier. Instead of barring the tides, as did the Haringvliet Dam, the Eastern Scheldt Dam would have enormous sluice gates to permit the natural ebb and flow of the tides. However, at the threat of rising seas, the 500-ton sluice gates—even larger than those of the Haringvliet—could be shut. Scrapping the original plan and substituting the storm-surge barrier tripled the cost of the entire Delta Project, which will eventually total some $4.5 billion, or roughly $325 for every Dutch citizen.

Construction of the complex structure on the unstable bed of the Eastern Scheldt sent Delta Project engineers back to their drawing boards to design a fleet of specialized vessels. In 1976, when construction began, a rig called the *Mytilus,* the Latin word for "mussel," prepared the sea bed. Beneath the 12-story-tall ship, four vibrating steel tubes plunged as much as 50 feet into the sea floor, compacting the sand and increasing its bearing capacity. At that point, a ship called the *Cardium,* Latin for "cockle," took over; its role was to lay 500-ton prefabricated mats of steel, synthetic fabric and rock in order to further stabilize the sand. Where conditions required, a floating asphalt factory deposited layers of asphalt.

In two cofferdam enclosures 50 feet below sea level, 66 concrete piers, measuring 131 feet in height and weighing 18,000 tons apiece, were built to support the massive steel sluice gates. When each set of piers was completed, its cofferdam was flooded. A horseshoe-shaped vessel called the *Ostrea,* or "oyster," then straddled the piers, hoisted them, and ferried them into the channel. There, shipboard computers guided them to within six inches of the design position.

The entire Delta Project, scheduled for completion in the late 1980s, calls for labor on a scale unprecedented in the history of public works. For the Netherlands, it represents a solution to the increasingly common problem of safeguarding people and property at the sea's edge while protecting natural environments such as the Eastern Scheldt estuary. But, as the leviathan concrete battlements along Dutch shores testify, the cost of the temporary victory has been—and may always be—dismayingly high. Ω

The Haringvliet Dam diverts the seaward flow of three Dutch rivers northward to the Rotterdam Waterway in order to flush silt from that shipping channel. When the rivers flood, the Haringvliet's 17 pairs of 180-foot-wide sluice gates swing open and allow the excess water to be released into the North Sea.

PICTURE CREDITS

The sources for the illustrations that appear in this book are listed below. Credits from left to right are separated by semicolons, from top to bottom by dashes.

Cover: NOAA. 6-15: Reg Morrison, *Australia, The Greatest Island: An Aerial Exploration of the Australian Coastline,* published by Lansdowne Press, Sydney. 16: Aerofilms, Hertfordshire, England. 18: Map by Bill Hezlep, after maps of Hans-Günter Gierloff-Emden and Cuchlaine A. M. King. 20: NASA. 22: NOAA. 24, 25: Dorothy Oldham © National Geographic Society, inset, James R. Root © National Geographic Society. 26: Art by Greg Harlin. 28, 29: Paul Jeffrey Godfrey. 30, 31: Art by Greg Harlin. 33: Jacob H. Kahn, courtesy National Ocean Survey/NOAA, Center for Wetland Resources/Louisiana State University and Department of Environmental Sciences/University of Virginia. 34, 35: © Gregory Heisler. 36, 37: Courtesy Kiawah Island Company. 38, 39: William Felger from Grant Heilman Photography. 40, 41: Klaus D. Francke, Hamburg. 42: Elton Welke—Aerofilms, Hertfordshire, England. 43: Ed Cooper. 44, 45: Peter Tenzer from Wheeler Pictures. 46, 47: Tad Nichols—Breck P. Kent; G. R. Roberts, Nelson, New Zealand. 48: Rolland A. Meyers. 50: Art by Greg Harlin. 51: G. R. Roberts, Nelson, New Zealand. 52: Cotton Coulson © 1982 from Woodfin Camp, Inc. 54, 55: British Tourist Authority, London—R. K. Pils-

bury, Isle of Wight, England. 56: Arthur Zich. 58-60: Art by Greg Harlin. 62, 63: © Steve Lissau. 65: © Richard Buettner. 67: Anne Wertheim © 1983—art by Greg Harlin. 68: Lynn M. Stone from Animals Animals. 69: © Jeff Rotman from Peter Arnold, Inc. 70, 71: National Park Service Photo by M. Woodbridge Williams. 72, 73: Lino Pellegrini, Milan. 74, 75: Stephen J. Krasemann from DRK Photo; © David M. Stone—Pierre Petit-Jacana, Paris. 76, 77: Tui De Roy Moore; Lanceau-Nature, Chamalières, France. 79: Baron Wolman © 1982 from Woodfin Camp & Associates. 80-91: Anne Wertheim © 1983. 92: Earth Satellite Corp. 95: John Lemker. 96, 97: Cotton Coulson © 1981 from Woodfin Camp & Associates. 98: Map by Bill Hezlep—Laboratoire Central d'Hydraulique de France, Maisons-Alfort, France. 100, 101: © Robert Frerck from Click/Chicago. 103: Art by Rob Wood. 106, 107: W. H. Watters. 108: Runk/Schoenberger from Grant Heilman Photography. 109: © Jack Wilburn from Earth Scenes. 110: © Bob Jones Jr. from Woodfin Camp, Inc.—Art by Biruta Akerbergs. 111: Robert W. Madden. 112: Art by Biruta Akerbergs. 114: Alex S. MacLean © 1983. 116, 117: José Dupont-Explorer, Paris. 118: Prof. Dr. Berndt Heydemann/Dr. Jutta Müller-Karch, Zoologisches Institut University of Kiel, Federal Republic of Germany. 119: Art by Rob Wood. 120, 121: Barrie Rokeach ©

1980. 122, 123: © Randy Brandon/Third Eye Photography. 124: William R. Curtsinger © National Geographic Society. 125: Grant Heilman. 126, 127: Reg Morrison, *Australia, The Greatest Island: An Aerial Exploration of the Australian Coastline,* published by Lansdowne Press, Sydney, inset, G. R. Roberts, Nelson, New Zealand. 128: R. Truchot-Explorer, Paris. 129: Klaus D. Francke, Hamburg. 130, 131: Aerofilms, Hertfordshire, England. 134, 135: Antonio Camoyán from Biofoto, Seville. 136, 137: Herminio M. Muñiz, Seville—Giuliano Cappelli, Florence; Antonio Camoyán from Biofoto, Seville (2). 138, 139: Jacques Robert-Jacana, Paris—Herminio M. Muñiz, Seville; Antonio Camoyán from Biofoto, Seville. 140, 141: Juan A. Fernández, Seville. 142: Ernst Haas. 144: Map by Bill Hezlep. 147: Fulvio Roiter, Venice. 148, 149: Dmitri Kessel, Paris, for *Smithsonian.* 150: Martin Rogers © 1979 from Woodfin Camp, Inc. 151: John Launois © 1978 from Black Star. 154, 155: Bart Hofmeester/Aerocamera, Rotterdam, inset, A. Van Pagee, Middelburg, the Netherlands. 157: Map by Bill Hezlep. 160, 161: © H. W. Silvester from Photo Researchers, Inc., inset, Orion Press from Bruce Coleman, Ltd., Middlesex, England. 162: © Ian Berry from Magnum. 163: KLM Aerocarto, Amsterdam. 165: Rijkswaterstaat Deltadienst, Zierikzee, the Netherlands. 166-169: KLM Aerocarto, Amsterdam.

BIBLIOGRAPHY

Books

Anikouchine, William A., and Richard W. Sternberg, *The World Ocean: An Introduction to Oceanography,* 2nd ed. Prentice-Hall, 1981.

Barnes, R.S.K., ed., *The Coastline.* John Wiley & Sons, 1977.

Bascom, Willard, *Waves and Beaches: The Dynamics of the Ocean Surface.* Anchor Press/Doubleday, 1980.

Berrill, N. J. and Jacquelyn, *1001 Questions Answered about the Seashore.* Dover Publications, 1976.

Bird, E.C.F., *Coasts: An Introduction to Systematic Geomorphology,* Vol. 4. M.I.T. Press, 1969.

Birkeland, Peter W., and Edwin E. Larson, *Putnam's Geology,* 3rd ed. Oxford University Press, 1978.

Borgese, Elisabeth Mann, *Seafarm: The Story of Aquaculture.* Harry N. Abrams, 1980.

Botting, Douglas, and the Editors of Time-Life Books, *Wilderness Europe.* Amsterdam: Time-Life Books, 1976.

Burton, Robert, *The Seashore and its Wildlife.* Putnam's, 1977.

Carefoot, Thomas, *Pacific Seashores: A Guide to Intertidal Ecology.* University of Washington Press, 1979.

Carson, Rachel:
The Edge of the Sea. New American Library, 1955.
The Rocky Coast. McCall Publishing, 1971.

Chapman, Abel, and Walter J. Buck:
Unexplored Spain. Madrid: Incafo, 1978.
Wild Spain. London: Gurney & Jackson, 1893.

Crosland, Patrick D., *The Outer Banks.* Interpretive Publications, 1981.

Davies, J. L., *Geographical Variation in Coastal Development.* Longman, 1980.

Dawes, Clinton J., *Marine Botany.* John Wiley & Sons, 1981.

De Combray, Richard, *Venice: Frail Barrier.* Doubleday, 1975.

Fay, Stephen, and Phillip Knightley, *The Death of Venice.* Praeger, 1976.

Fernández, Juan Antonio, *Doñana: Spain's Wildlife Wilderness.* Taplinger Publishing, 1975.

Giddings, J. Louis, *Ancient Men of the Arctic.* Alfred A. Knopf, 1967.

Gresswell, R. Kay, *The Physical Geography of Beaches and Coastlines.* London: Hulton Educational Publi-

cations, 1957.

Gross, M. Grant, *Oceanography: A View of the Earth.* Prentice-Hall, 1980.

Hewlett, Stefani, and K. Gilbey, *Sea Life of the Pacific Northwest.* McGraw-Hill Ryerson, 1976.

Hoyt, John H., *Field Guide to Beaches.* Houghton Mifflin, 1971.

Idyll, C. P., *The Sea Against Hunger.* Thomas Y. Crowell, 1978.

Kaufman, Wallace, and Orrin Pilkey, *The Beaches Are Moving: The Drowning of America's Shoreline.* Anchor Press/Doubleday, 1979.

Keast, Allen, *Australia and the Pacific Islands.* Random House, 1966.

Ketchum, Bostwick H., ed., *The Water's Edge: Critical Problems of the Coastal Zone.* M.I.T. Press, 1972.

King, Cuchlaine A. M., *Beaches and Coasts.* St. Martin's Press, 1972.

Klingel, Gilbert C.:
The Bay. Tradition Press, 1967.
Seeing Chesapeake Wilds. International Marine Publishing, 1970.

Komar, Paul D., *Beach Processes and Sedimentation.* Prentice-Hall, 1976.

Koning, Hans, and the Editors of Time-Life Books, *Amsterdam.* Amsterdam: Time-Life International, 1977.

Kopper, Philip, *The Wild Edge: Life and Lore of the Great Atlantic Beaches.* Penguin Books, 1981.

Kozloff, Eugene, *Seashore Life of Puget Sound, the Strait of Georgia, and the San Juan Archipelago.* University of Washington Press, 1973.

Lane, Frederic C., *Venice: A Maritime Republic.* Johns Hopkins University Press, 1973.

Lauff, George H., ed., *Estuaries.* American Association for the Advancement of Science, 1967.

Limburg, Peter R., *Farming the Waters.* Beaufort Books, 1980.

Lippson, Alice Jane, ed., *The Chesapeake Bay in Maryland: An Atlas of Natural Resources.* Johns Hopkins University Press, 1973.

MacGinitie, G. E. and Nettie, *Natural History of Marine Animals.* McGraw-Hill, 1968.

Manley, Seon and Robert, *Beaches: Their Lives, Legends, and Lore.* Chilton Book Company, 1968.

Menen, Aubrey, and the Editors of Time-Life Books,

Venice. Amsterdam: Time-Life International, 1976.

Mountfort, Guy, *Portrait of a Wilderness: The Story of the Coto Doñana Expeditions.* London: Hutchinson, 1958.

Oldale, Robert N., *Geologic History of Cape Cod, Massachusetts.* U.S. Government Printing Office, 1981.

Pilkey, Orrin H., Jr., William J. Neal, Orrin H. Pilkey Sr. and Stanley R. Riggs, *From Currituck to Calabash: Living with North Carolina's Barrier Islands.* North Carolina Science and Technology Research Center, 1980.

Press, Frank, and Raymond Siever, *Earth.* W. H. Freeman, 1982.

Raymond, Robert, *Australia, The Greatest Island: An Aerial Exploration of the Australian Coastline.* Lansdowne Press, 1979.

Reinhardt, Richard, Michael Goodwin, Tom Johnson and John Burks, *California from the Air: The Golden Coast.* Squarebooks, 1981.

Ricketts, Edward F., and Jack Calvin, *Between Pacific Tides.* Stanford University Press, 1968.

Ritter, Dale F., *Process Geomorphology.* Wm. C. Brown, 1978.

Roberts, Mervin F., *The Tidemarsh Guide.* E. P. Dutton, 1979.

Russell, Richard J., *River Plains and Sea Coasts.* University of California Press, 1967.

Sargent, William, *Shallow Waters: A Year on Cape Cod's Pleasant Bay.* Houghton Mifflin, 1981.

Schubel, J. R., *The Living Chesapeake.* Johns Hopkins University Press, 1981.

Shepard, Francis P., and Harold R. Wanless, *Our Changing Coastlines.* McGraw-Hill, 1971.

Schwartz, Maurice L., ed., *Barrier Islands.* Dowden, Hutchinson & Ross, 1973.

Simon, Anne W., *The Thin Edge: Coast and Man in Crisis.* Avon Books, 1979.

Snead, Rodman E., *Coastal Landforms and Surface Features: A Photographic Atlas and Glossary.* Hutchinson Ross, 1982.

Spier, Peter, *Of Dikes and Windmills.* Doubleday, 1969.

Stephens, William M., *Southern Seashores: A World of Animals and Plants.* Holiday House, 1968.

Stick, David, *The Outer Banks of North Carolina.* University of North Carolina Press, 1958.

Stone, Carolyn R., *Australian Landforms*. Wren Publishing, 1974.

Stonehouse, Bernard, *Britain from the Air*. Crown Publishers, 1982.

Teal, John and Mildred, *Life and Death of the Salt Marsh*. Little, Brown, 1969.

Thubron, Colin, and the Editors of Time-Life Books, *The Venetians*. Time-Life Books, 1980.

Thurman, Harold V., *Introductory Oceanography*. Charles E. Merrill, 1981.

Van Andel, Tjeerd, *Tales of an Old Ocean*. W. W. Norton, 1978.

Venice: Complete Guide in Colour. Venice: Edizioni Storti, 1978.

Warner, William W., *Beautiful Swimmers: Watermen, Crabs and the Chesapeake Bay*. Penguin Books, 1976.

Weber, Karl, and Lukas Hoffman, *Camargue: The Soul of a Wilderness*. Transl. by Ewald Osers. Joseph J. Binns, 1977.

Wylie, Francis E., *Tides and the Pull of the Moon*. Stephen Greene Press, 1979.

Zanzotto, Andrea, *Living Venice*. Udine: Magnus Edizioni, 1978.

Zenkovich, V. P., *Processes of Coastal Development*. Ed. by J. A. Steers, transl. by D. G. Fry. London: Oliver & Boyd, 1967.

Zim, Herbert S., and Lester Ingle, *Seashores: A Guide to Animals and Plants along the Beaches*. Golden Press, 1955.

Periodicals

Allen, Frank, "Muddy Waters: Dying or Evolving, the Chesapeake Bay Shows Signs of Stress." *The Wall Street Journal*, September 27, 1982.

"Amoco Cadiz: A Lasting Disaster." *Science News*, August 5, 1978.

Apple, R. W., Jr., "Dutch Are Spending Billions on a Project to Keep Sea at Bay." *The New York Times*, October 25, 1981.

Behn, Robert D., and Martha A. Clark, "The Termination of Beach Erosion Control at Cape Hatteras." *Public Policy*, Winter 1979.

Bennett, D. W., "Magic Beaches: No." *Water Spectrum*, Summer 1978.

Black, Ann, "Cape Lookout: A Voyage to Discovery." *National Parks & Conservation Magazine*, July 1980.

Blackford, Frank, "The Sea Is Just a Step Away." *The Virginian Pilot Lighthouse*, December 17, 1972.

Clark, Blake, "Holland's Greatest Disaster since the Middle Ages." *The Reader's Digest*, August 1953.

Davenport, William, "The Camargue: France's Wild, Watery South." *National Geographic*, May 1973.

De Cessole, Bruno, "Venice: Can It Still Be Saved?" Transl. from *Ça M'Interesse*, January 1983.

Doidge, Pauline, "The Drowning of Venice." *New Scientist*, June 17, 1982.

Dolan, Robert, and Bruce Hayden, "Adjusting to Nature in Our National Seashores." *National Parks & Conservation Magazine*, June 1974.

Dolan, Robert, Bruce Hayden and Harry Lins, "Barrier Islands." *American Scientist*, January/February 1980.

Dolan, Robert, Paul J. Godfrey and William E. Odum, "Man's Impact on the Barrier Islands of North Carolina." *American Scientist*, March/April 1973.

Ellis, Carolyn, "Working on the Bay." *Southern Exposure*, May/June 1982.

Ellis, Harry B., "Huge Dutch Barriers to Block Off North Sea." *The Christian Science Monitor*, October 21, 1969.

Emiliani, Cesare, "Ice Sheets and Ice Melts." *Natural History*, November 1980.

Flemming, Carrol B., "Muddy Waters: The Hidden Bay." *Science 82*, October 1982.

Gatto, P., and L. Carbognin, "The Lagoon of Venice: Natural Environmental Trend and Man-Induced Modification." *Hydrological Sciences Bulletin*, December 1981.

Gierloff-Emden, Hans-Günter, "Nehrungen und Lagunen." *Petermanns Geographische Mitteilungen*, 1961, 3rd quarter.

Goodspeed, Tom, "Barrier Island Bass." *Outdoor Life*, May 1982.

Haedrich, R. L., and C.A.S. Hall, "Fishes and Estuaries." *Oceanus*, Fall 1976.

Halperin, David, "Dutch Delta Dikes: Locking Out the Ocean, Locking Up the Rhine." *Oceans*, March/April 1980.

Hamblin, Dora Jane, "Maladies of Venice: Decay, Delay and that Old Sinking Feeling." *Smithsonian*, November 1977.

Hendrikse, Dick, "They Made a Living Dike." *Reader's Digest*, June 1953.

Hitchcock, Stephen, "Can We Save Our Salt Marshes?" *National Geographic*, June 1972.

Inman, Douglas L., and Birchard M. Brush, "The Coastal Challenge." *Science*, July 1973.

Jerome, Lawrence E., "Marsh Restorations." *Oceans*, January/February 1979.

Judge, Joseph, "Venice Fights for Life." *National Geographic*, November 1972.

Kenney, Nathaniel T., and B. Anthony Stewart, "Our Changing Atlantic Coastline." *National Geographic*, December 1962.

Koenig, Peter, "Remember the Amoco Cadiz." *Audubon*, March 1981.

Lansford, Ruth L., "The Ballona Wetlands." *Oceans*, January/February 1979.

MacIntyre, Ferren, "Why the Sea Is Salt." *Scientific American*, November 1970.

MacLeish, William H., "Our Barrier Islands Are the Key Issue in 1980, the 'Year of the Coast.'" *Smithsonian*, September 1980.

Miller, H. Crane, "A Gamble with Time and Nature: The Barrier Islands." *Environment*, November 1981.

Moore, Peter, et al., "Côto de Doñana: Survival of a Wilderness." *New Scientist*, November 11, 1982.

North, Wheeler J., "Giant Kelp: Sequoias of the Sea." *National Geographic*, August 1972.

Oceans, January 1968-November/December 1982.

Oceanus, Winter 1952-Winter 1982.

Pilkey, Orrin H., "America's Beaches: An Endangered Species?" *Sea Grant Today*, November/December 1981.

Ricciuti, Edward R.:
"The Harvest in the Deep." *Geo*, May 1981.
"The Land between the Tides." *Geo*, March 1982.

Rockefeller, Laurance, "The Great Barrier Island Bailout." *National Parks & Conservation Magazine*, July 1980.

Silberner, Joanne, "Hold that Line!" *Science News*, January 17, 1981.

Soucie, Gary, "Where the Beaches Have Been Going: Into the Ocean—Ironically Hastened by Man-made Remedies." *Smithsonian*, June 1973.

Sparrow, Susan, "Barriers—the Inconstant Lands." *National Parks & Conservation Magazine*, July 1980.

Tarpy, Cliff, "The Beauty and the Battle of San Francisco Bay." *National Geographic*, June 1981.

Thomsen, Dietrick E., "Life on the Shifting Sands." *Science News*, February 25, 1978.

"Too Many Flamingoes or Too Much Rain?" *Bulletin of Regional Nature Park of the Camargue*, September 1978.

Underwater Naturalist, November 1962-Summer 1982.

"Venice Rises above a Sea of Troubles." *U.S. News & World Report*, May 31, 1982.

"The Wrath of a Nameless Storm Out of Nowhere." *Life*, March 19, 1962.

Other Publications

Coates, Donald R., ed., *Coastal Geomorphology*. A proceedings volume of the Third Annual Geomorphology Symposia Series, held at Binghamton, New York, September 28-30, 1972. State University of New York, Binghamton, 1972.

A Compact Geography of the Netherlands. Compiled by the Information and Documentation Centre for the Geography of the Netherlands at the request of the Ministry of Foreign Affairs. The Hague/Utrecht, 1974.

Deep-Compaction Oosterschelde Storm Surge Barrier. Ministry of Transport and Public Works, Deltaworks Department (Rijkswaterstaat), Holland, no date.

Dolan, Robert, and Robert Linn, *Dune Stabilization and Beach Erosion: Cape Hatteras National Seashore, North Carolina*. Dune Stabilization Study, 1972.

Dolan, Robert, Bruce Hayden and Jeffrey Heywood, *Atlas of Environmental Dynamics: Assateague Island National Seashore*. Natural Resource Report No. 11, October 1977. Department of Environmental Sciences of the University of Virginia, Charlottesville.

Dolan, Robert, Harry Lins and John Stewart, *Geographical Analysis of Fenwick Island, Maryland, a Middle Atlantic Coast Barrier Island*. Geological Survey Professional Paper 1177-A, U.S. Government Printing Office, 1980.

The Estuarine Environment: Estuaries and Estuarine Sedimentation. Short Course Lecture Notes, Wye Institute, October 30-31, 1971. American Geological Institute, 1971.

Fairbridge, Rhodes W., "The Estuary: Its Definition and Geodynamic Cycle." Chapter 1 of *Chemistry and Biogeochemistry of Estuaries*. E. Olausson and I. Cato, eds. John Wiley & Sons, 1980.

Munk, Judith and Walter, *Venice Hologram*. Read April 21, 1972, at the Scripps Institute of Oceanography, University of California. Published in the Proceedings of the American Philosophical Society, Vol. 116, No. 5, October 1972.

ACKNOWLEDGMENTS

For their help in the preparation of this book the editors wish to thank: **In Australia:** Sydney—Anne Wilson, Managing Editor, Lansdowne Editions. **In France:** Arles—Jacqueline Gagneron, Parc Naturel Régional de la Camargue; Rémy Bühler, Syndicat des Vignerons de la Région d'Arles; Caen—Claude Larsonneur, Laboratoire de Géologie Marine, Université de Caen; Maisons-Alfort—Bertrand Bellesort, Claude Migniot, Laboratoire Central d'Hydraulique de France. **In the German Democratic Republic:** Gotha—Dr. Franz Köhler, VEB Hermann Haack, Geographisch-Kartographische Anstalt. **In Italy:** Venice—Marina Magrini, Luigi Scanno, Comune di Venezia; Contessa Teresa Foscolo Foscari, Roberto Frassetto, Paolo Gatto, Istituto per lo Studio della Dinamica delle Grandi Masse, CNR. **In the United States:** Alaska—(Kotzebue) C. Mack Shaver, Superintendent, Cape Krusenstern National Monument; California—(Santa Cruz) Dr. Gary Griggs, Department of Earth Sciences, University of California; Florida—(Miami) Dr. Scott E. Siddall, School of Marine and Atmospheric Science, University of Miami; Hawaii—Dr. Robert Decker, Hawaiian Volcano Observatory; Maryland—(Annapolis) Vicky Seymour, Maryland Office of Tourist Development; Greg Harlin, Rob Wood, Stansbury, Ronsaville, Wood, Inc.; (Shady Side) Dr. Walter Taylor, Chesapeake Bay Institute, The Johns Hopkins University; New Mexico—(Albuquerque) Dr. Rodman E. Snead, Department of Geography, University of New Mexico; New York—(New York) Dr. Rhodes W. Fairbridge; (Stony Brook) Dr. Donald W.

Pritchard, Associate Director for Research, State University of New York; (Syracuse) Dr. Edward Muir, Department of History, Syracuse University; North Carolina—(Durham) Dr. Orrin H. Pilkey Jr., Geology Department, Duke University; (Manteo) Robert Woody, Cape Hatteras National Seashore; Bud Cannon, Dare County Tourist Bureau; (Roanoke Island) Rhett B. White, Marine Resources Center; Oregon—(Corvallis) Dr. Paul D. Komar, School of Oceanography, Oregon State University; (Newport) Dr. Jefferson J. Gonor, Marine Science Center; Texas—(Dallas) Dr. Donald Swift, ARCO Oil & Gas; (Fort Worth) Dr. John G. McPherson, Department of Geology, University of Texas; Virginia—(Burke) Bill Hezlep; (Charlottesville) Nina Fisher, Dr. Jacob Kahn, Wilma LeVan, Department of Environmental Sciences, University of Virginia; (Gloucester Point) Sue Gammisch, Virginia Institute of Marine Science; Washington—(Bellingham) Dr. Maurice L.

Schwartz, Department of Geology, Western Washington University; (Seattle) Dr. Ronald Phillips, School of Natural and Mathematical Sciences, Seattle Pacific University. **In West Germany:** Kiel—Dr. Berndt Heydemann, Zoologisches Institut, Universität Kiel; Munich—Dr. H. G. Gierloff-Emden; West Berlin—Dr. Roland Klemig, Heidi Klein, Bildarchiv Preussischer Kulturbesitz; Wolfgang Streubel, Ullstein Bilderdienst.

The editors also wish to thank the following persons: Mirka Gondicas, Athens; Robert Gilmore, Auckland; Lois Lorimer, Copenhagen; Scott Horton, Ecuador; Bing Wong, Hong Kong; Robert W. Bone, Honolulu; Martha de la Cal, Lisbon; Kazuo Ohyauchi, Tokyo.

Particularly useful sources of information and quotations used in this volume were: *Australia, The Greatest Island: An Aerial Exploration of the Australian Coastline* by Robert Raymond, Lansdowne Press, 1979; *Beautiful Swimmers: Watermen, Crabs and the*

Chesapeake Bay by William W. Warner, Penguin Books, 1976; *Beach Processes and Sedimentation* by Paul D. Komar, Prentice-Hall, 1976; *The Beaches Are Moving: The Drowning of America's Shoreline* by Wallace Kaufman and Orrin Pilkey, Anchor Press/Doubleday, 1979; *Coasts: An Introduction to Systematic Geomorphology*, Vol. 4, by E.C.F. Bird, M.I.T. Press, 1969; *From Currituck to Calabash: Living with North Carolina's Barrier Islands* by Orrin H. Pilkey Jr., William J. Neal, Orrin H. Pilkey Sr. and Stanley R. Riggs, North Carolina Science and Technology Research Center, 1980; *Introductory Oceanography* by Harold V. Thurman, Charles E. Merrill, 1981; *Pacific Seashores: A Guide to Intertidal Ecology* by Thomas Carefoot, University of Washington Press, 1979; *The Seashore and its Wildlife* by Robert Burton, Putnam's, 1977; *The Wild Edge: Life and Lore of the Great Atlantic Beaches* by Philip Kopper, Penguin Books, 1981.

The index was prepared by Gisela S. Knight.

INDEX